HIGH IMPACT RESUMES & LETTERS

Fourth Edition

WITHDRAWN

Ronald L. Krannich, Ph.D.
William J. Banis, M.A.

IMPACT PUBLICATIONS
Woodbridge, VA

HIGH IMPACT RESUMES AND LETTERS: How to Communicate Your Qualifications to Employers

Fourth Edition

Library of Congress Cataloguing-in-Publication Data

Krannich, Ronald L.
   High impact resumes and letters

        Bibliography: p.
        Includes index.
        1. Resumes (Employment)   2. Commercial correspondence.
I. Banis, William J. II. Title.
HF5383.K7   1990   650.1'4   90-4223
ISBN 0-942710-30-4

For information on distribution or quantity discount rates, Tel. 703/361-7300, FAX 703/335-9486, or write to: Sales Department, IMPACT PUBLICATIONS, 4580 Sunshine Court, Woodbridge, VA 22192. Distributed to the trade by National Book Network, 4720 Boston Way, Suite A, Lanham, MD 20706, Tel. 301/459-8696.

TABLE OF CONTENTS

PREFACE

Whether you are first entering, re-entering, or changing jobs and careers within the job market, there's a 90 percent chance you will join millions of other job seekers in sending resumes and letters to more than one potential employer. How well you both write and distribute your resume and letters will largely determine if you will receive an invitation to interview for a job you really want.

Resumes and job search letters may well be the most important written communication of your life. Failure to communicate your qualifications loud and clear to employers will affect your future job satisfaction, career advancement, and potential earnings.

Few people know the secrets to writing high impact resumes and letters. Lacking clear goals, strong organization, and a sense of direction in their job search, they founder in the job market with poorly written resumes and letters that communicate their weaknesses rather than demonstrate their strengths. Not surprisingly, they receive few invitations for job interviews.

However, a growing number of our readers have learned how to better organize and target their job search by following the practical resume and letter advice offered in our past three editions of this book. Unlike many other books on resumes and letters, this book walks you through two closely linked processes simultaneously in order to develop powerful communication skills: the job search process and the resume and letter writing process. We don't just show you how to write nice looking resumes and letters. We also show you how to market and manage your written communication for maximum impact. Thus, when you finish this book, you should be in a much better position to open the doors of potential employers and get those interviews that lead to excellent job offers and satisfying jobs.

This fourth edition of *High Impact Resumes and Letters* again places resumes and letters within the larger job search and career planning processes. Based on years of experience in training and counseling thousands of job seekers as well as writing, revising, and reviewing hundreds of resumes, we've learned the best resumes and letters -- those that move employers to interview the *"best qualified"* candidates -- must reflect the *"unique you"*. If written according to our advice, such resumes and letters will clearly communicate your goals as well as your patterns of skills and achievements to employers who want to minimize the risks of hiring strangers. Such resumes and letters translate your goals, skills, and achievements as being the employer's hiring needs. They tell employers that you are someone who has the best potential for solving their present and future problems.

If this is your first job search book, you may find it addresses many more questions than just how to write effective resumes and letters. Indeed, this edition of *High Impact Resumes and Letters* includes, in the form of a review essay (Chapter Twelve), an analysis of the most important resources for finding jobs and changing careers. If, for example, you feel you need more information on assessing your skills, setting goals, conducting job research, networking, interviewing, or negotiating salaries, you may find this new section especially useful. In keeping with our emphasis on the practical, we also include information on how to acquire these resources (page 245) as well as receive a free catalog of nearly 1,000 annotated career resources (page 6). The catalog will give you both an overview of the major job and career resources available today and access to the ones that may best meet your particular needs.

Join us as we take you on an important journey into what should become one of the most exciting and rewarding adventures of a lifetime -- communicating your qualifications to employers who, in turn, will invite you to job interviews. If you follow this book carefully and implement each chapter, you should join thousands of our other readers who report greater success in their job search efforts.

We wish you the very best as you create your own high impact resumes and letters. Whatever you do, make sure your written job search communication has impact. If you can achieve such impact, you will be well on your way to increased job and career success!

Chapter One

PUT IMPACT INTO YOUR COMMUNICATIONS

Regardless of what others may tell you, expertly crafted and intelligently distributed resumes and letters do lead to job interviews that eventually turn into job offers and satisfying jobs. But not everyone knows the secrets to creating and using high impact resumes and letters. That's our task in the following pages -- to show you how to put the maximum *impact* into your written job search communications so that you can get the job you want.

FOCUS ON THE PROCESS

Please be forewarned that this is not your normal reflective resume and letter writing guidebook crammed with examples of *"good"* resumes and letters. The market is full of such guides that assume you can write good resumes and letters through a process of emulation or osmosis. Just visit your local bookstore or library and you will be assaulted with such books of examples. Most of these guides present the final products with little useful advice on how you get to point A -- identifying your goals -- and then proceed on to points B, C, D, E, and F -- skills, experience, organizations, jobs, and employers.

1

This is a different book. It's designed to put you to work creating and distributing your own high impact resumes and letters. Our focus is on the job finding *process*. We stress the importance of having explicit goals and strong organization for achieving the most desired job search outcomes -- job interviews and offers. For many of our readers, implementing this book has become a very rewarding experience. They've traveled along the road to discover their *"real self"* as well as communicated their qualifications loud and clear to potential employers.

Indeed, we don't just explain how to write so-called effective resumes and letters and then pad the book with lots of unrelated examples that may or may not be relevant to your situation. Instead, we take you on an important journey of self-discovery as you explore the *"ins"* and *"outs"* of one of the most important steps in any job search. We show you how this step is critically related to other equally important steps as you get on track to achieving job search success. We'll show you not only how to *write* powerful resumes and letters but also how, when, and where to *distribute* them for maximum impact. When you finish this book, you will be in a powerful position to get the job you want.

Most important of all, you will learn how to *present your best self* prior to being invited to a formal job interview. While this may not be an easy task, it is much less painful than many people believe it is, or make it to be. For in creating high impact resumes and letters you also present an image of yourself that helps direct every stage of your job search. As such, writing and distributing high impact resumes and letters should become central activities in your whole job search.

ANYONE CAN FIND A JOB

It's no big secret. Almost anyone can find a job. But finding a really good job -- one you do well, enjoy doing, and look forward to each day as well as see yourself doing for many years to come -- is not the usual outcome of most job searches. People find jobs, leave jobs, and go looking for other jobs in a cycle of job-hopping that is common-place in our employment culture. Part of the reason for making these changes goes back to the methods people use for finding and keeping jobs, from the very moment they write a resume to when they negotiate a job offer.

Finding a good job involves much more than responding to want ads with pieces of paper called resumes and letters. Above all, it requires you to communicate your qualifications to employers in the most efficient and effective manner possible. Resumes and letters are only two means --

albeit the most popular and frequently used -- of doing so. Whether they are efficient and effective depends on both *what* you communicate and *how* you communicate your message.

Rather than dismiss resumes and letters as ineffective ways of finding jobs, you should learn how to best develop and target your written communication in conjunction with other forms of communication for maximum impact on employers. That is the subject of this book. Indeed, communicating your qualifications to employers is one of the most important tasks in your job search. Everything you do -- be it identifying your skills, formulating an objective, conducting job research, writing resumes and letters, or networking for information -- should be aimed at linking your capabilities to employers' needs.

> *Finding a good job . . . requires you to communicate your qualifications to employers in the most efficient and effective manner possible . . . Everything you do . . . should be aimed at linking your capabilities to employers' needs.*

IT'S ALL ABOUT BEING EFFECTIVE

Communication in the job market is all about being effective -- having a positive impact on employers and your employment future. You want others to take action that will result in a really good job.

To be most effective, you must formulate a high quality *message* and then *disseminate* it through specific *communication channels*. In so doing, you develop *strategies* -- either implicitly or explicitly -- for communicating your message to employers.

The message, channels, and strategies come together in a well defined *process* when you write resumes and letters. This process -- the formulation and dissemination of formal written communication -- plays a critical role in your overall job search. You must write high quality resumes and letters because you want to:

1. Uncover job leads
2. Gain access to employers
3. Succinctly communicate the *"unique you"* to employers

Without such resumes and letters, you will have difficulty gaining access and communicating your qualifications to employers. Above all, resumes and letters lend legitimacy to your job search as well as provide you and employers with a central focal point for examining your qualifications. If you develop high quality messages and disseminate them properly, you will indeed communicate your qualifications to employers with impact.

Resumes and letters . . . are wonderful two-edge swords for cutting through other less organized forms of communication.

PRODUCTS PROMOTING A PROCESS

The purpose of this book is to clarify how you can make this process work for you -- from beginning to end. Let's be perfectly clear what we are and are not doing here. We emphasize the whole *process* rather than examine only a few discrete elements within the process. We provide examples of resumes and letters but only within the context of the larger career planning and job search processes as well as in direct reference to the principles of writing different types of resumes and letters.

Resumes and job search letters are some of the most controversial and abused forms of communication. Most career counselors, for example, advise you to write a one to two-page resume and use it frequently throughout your job search. Others claim resumes are unnecessary and thus you should use alternative means of communication, especially networking, to gain access to employers. Still others concentrate on developing individual resume elements with little regard for the function and use of resumes in the overall job search process.

Frankly, there is a lot of nonsense written about resumes and letters by people who should know better -- or better know what goes on in the job search process. This book is based upon a very simple fact of employment life: *resumes and letters are important parts of the job search process which are here to stay.* They are here to stay because they are wonderful two-edge swords for cutting through other less organized forms of communication: employers find them efficient for screening candidates; candidates know they are accepted passcards for opening the doors of employers.

Resumes and letters are written products to be used in furthering an important process.

Put another way, resumes and letters are written *products* to be used in furthering an important *process*. If written well and used intelligently, they can open the doors to job and career success. If written poorly and used inappropriately, resumes will be useless, if not negative, for one's job search campaign.

USE THE RIGHT RESOURCES

Each year millions of job hunters turn to career planning books for assistance. Normally they begin with a general book and next turn to resume and interview books.

If this book represents your first career planning and job search book, you may want to supplement it with a few other key books, especially our comprehensive career planning guide -- *Careering and Re-Careering for the 1990s*. This and many other books are available in your local library and bookstore, or they can be ordered directly from Impact Publications by completing the order form at the end of this book. As a user of this book, you are entitled to a free copy of the most comprehensive career catalog available today. To receive the latest edition of this catalog of nearly 1,000 annotated career resources, simply write or call:

IMPACT PUBLICATIONS
ATTN: Free Careers Catalog
4580 Sunshine Court
Woodbridge, VA 22192
Tel. 703/361-7300

They will send you a copy immediately upon request. Their catalog contains almost every important career and job finding resource available today, including many titles that are difficult, if not impossible, to find in bookstores and libraries. Included in this catalog are eight of our other career planning and job search titles that examine other critical steps in the job search process as well as careers in government and international affairs: *Careering and Re-Careering for the 1990s, Interview for Success, Network Your Way to Job and Career Success, Discover the Right Job for You, Salary Success, Find a Federal Job Fast, The Complete Guide to Public Employment*, and *The Complete Guide to International Jobs and Careers.*

Chapter Two

FROM RITUALS
TO WRITING RIGHT

So you're looking for a job. How do you plan to get one? Whom will you contact? How will you go about meeting potential employers? Will this be the right job for you? Do you really know what employers want from you? What will you do next?

Let's discuss some of these initial job search questions so we know we're going in the right direction and talking the same language about resumes, jobs, and employers.

GETTING STARTED

Let's look at the typical way most people go about writing resumes and letters and positioning them in the job market.

> *"I'm really excited about finding a job. What I thought I would do first is write my resume. That shouldn't take long — maybe two or three hours. Once I get it finished, I'll send it to employers along with a cover letter. Isn't that what most people do?"*

You're right. Most people do start with a resume. Perhaps you could expand a little more by explaining what you plan to put into your resume.

> *"I really haven't given that much thought. I have a copy of a friend's resume. She also loaned me a resume book filled with examples. I'll look at these examples for some guidance. I guess I'll include what most people put on their resumes -- education, work history, special interests, references, salary expectations. Isn't that what's supposed to go on a resume?"*

Yes, most resumes include much of that information. But we're more interested in how *you* will write, produce, and distribute *your* resume. What will your resume say about you in terms of your goals, strengths, and future productivity for the employer? How many pages will it be? How will you produce it? Will it be typed or typeset? What about the color and weight of the paper? How many copies will you run? Whom will you send it to? What type of response do you expect to receive? How long will you wait before you contact the employer about the status of your application? Indeed, you'll have to address many of these and other questions as you get into the details of writing and distributing your resume and letters.

> *"Yeah, that's a lot to think about. I haven't really given those questions much thought. I've been most concerned about just getting my resume written! I can see there are several things I need to consider once I finish writing my resume. Or maybe I need to answer those questions before I write my resume. What do you think?"*

We think you're beginning to ask the right questions. In fact, the solution to most problems is found in asking the right questions. If you ask the right questions about your resume, letters, and job search, chances are the answers will come much easier. But if you don't ask those questions up front, you may end up doing what so many other job seekers do -- head off with inappropriate baggage which results in conducting an ineffective job search. We think you can and should do better.

What we want you to do is consider writing high impact resumes and letters. These will take more than two or three hours to write, and they can not be written by just modifying examples. They require you to do first things first. And one of the first things you should *not* do is write a resume. If you are to write it right, you first need information about yourself and employers. This information will be the basis for carefully constructing each section of your resume.

More importantly, let's make an important strategic decision at this point: make your resume the central focus or driving force around which you will organize each step of your job search. In so doing, your resume becomes more than just a piece of paper for passing your history on to employers. Carefully crafted, it represents you, your job search, and your future. It's a particular type of product, based upon a well defined process, which should have a tremendous impact on your future.

Interested? Let's see what we can do in the next few hours to properly pack your bags as you journey along a new road to job and career success.

Make your resume the central focus or driving force around which you will organize each step of your job search.

THE CRITICAL DIFFERENCE

Each year millions of anxious souls engage in a curious paper ritual. They write resumes and cover letters, send them to prospective employers, and wait to be called for a job interview and/or receive a job offer. Some even hire a professional to write and distribute their resumes and letters -- thinking an expert might have better success than doing it themselves.

While most people hope to write resumes and letters which will put them on the road to job search success, few have the knack to put it all together with impact. But what exactly are high impact resumes and letters?

High impact resumes and letters are ones which grab the attention of employers who then invite you to an interview. They are an accurate representation of you, your strengths, and your future productivity. Communicating what it is you have done, can do, and will do, high impact resumes and letters make the critical difference between getting no response or getting a positive response. That positive response is an invitation to interview for a job which, in turn, may result in a job offer and a satisfying job.

> *High impact resumes and letters*
> *are ones that grab the attention*
> *of employers who then invite*
> *you to an interview.*

REVIEWING THE MAIL

Let's turn the tables for a moment to see exactly what is being communicated in today's world of work. Put yourself in the shoes of the employer who gets numerous resumes and letters. Suppose, for example, you received 150 resumes and letters this week in response to your vacancy announcement. After spending six hours sorting these paper qualifications into three piles -- *"yes"*, *"maybe"*, *"no"* -- you discover your stack of *"yeses"* is very thin. Most resumes found their way into your *"no"* pile where they quickly find their way into the trash can. In fact, 75 percent of these resumes and letters should never have been sent to you. Out of 150 resumes and letters, you have only found seven people that you will consider inviting for an interview. You'll telephone these candidates tomorrow to see if they *sound* as promising as they *look* on paper. Then you will be able to decide whom you wish to *see* in person.

Having gone through this sorting ritual, you reflect on the crucial resume and letter writing step in the job search. You're surprised:

1. How poorly people portray themselves on paper.
2. What they are willing to tell strangers who have the power to hire.
3. Why they think they can get a job primarily by using the postal system.

Is this the best they can do? After all, you are offering a good job with potential for career advancement -- your money for their talent. You would think applicants would be more serious about themselves, their futures, and employers' interests. If these resumes and letters are any indication, few seem to really care.

COMMUNICATION RITUALS

We're not anthropologists, but we know a communication ritual when we see one. Resume and letter writing is a kind of ritual, complete with a set of beliefs about how one should relate to the job world with pieces of paper for communicating one's qualifications to employers. As with most rituals, this one is a mixture of myths, magic, and mysterious movement. Thus, resume and letter writing becomes an accepted *"rite of passage"* in the process of finding a job.

Employers want to know what
you will do for them in the
future -- not your history.

While most people feel they must write resumes and letters to get a job, few fully understand what they are doing or how they can best improve their communication skills. Only some people know the secrets to creating and targeting high impact resumes and letters to the right people for achieving job search success.

Indeed, the way most people write and distribute resumes and letters in today's job market would lead one to believe they are not really serious about finding a job nor are they concerned about the needs of employers. After all, why would anyone develop a resume or write a letter based upon someone else's examples? Or why would someone just list employment dates, positions, and job duties and responsibilities on their resume? And some even go so far as to include such personal information as their height, weight, hobbies, and children! Have they no self-respect? Don't they know what they're doing? Have they no sense of focus? What is it they want -- other than this job? Don't they know employers have very specific needs?

Above all, employers want to know what you will do for them in the *future* -- not your history. That means you must clearly state an objective with corresponding capabilities relating to the employer's needs.

HIGH IMPACT COMMUNICATION

Few job seekers know how to write effective resumes and letters in today's job market. They have yet to learn the secrets to writing and distributing high impact resumes and letters.

To have impact in a sea of job search paper should be your single most important goal.

Since high impact resumes and letters are designed to grab the attention of employers and result in invitations to job interviews, these documents clearly communicate a message -- your qualifications -- in relation to employers' needs. In contrast to the *"canned"* language found in resumes and letters produced from others' examples, high impact resumes and letters tell employers that you have the requisite skills and abilities to do the job. Moreover, these resumes and letters persuade employers to invite you to an interview where you will be asked to elaborate on the content of your resume.

To have *impact* in a sea of job search paper should be your single most important goal when writing and distributing resumes and letters. For to produce ritual documents and distribute them in the traditional manner is the best way *not* to be taken seriously in today's job market.

SUCCESSFUL COMMUNICATION

Maybe you've wondered about differences in human abilities and how you compare to others. Why, for example, do some people know how to open the right doors to career success while others seem to struggle to get ahead? Are they more experienced or better qualified? Are they inherently more intelligent? Maybe they are just luckier. Or do they know something about the hiring process and employers that others do not?

Be it ability, intelligence, knowledge, or sheer luck, getting ahead in today's job market at the very least requires key *communication skills*. Indeed, successful job hunters -- those who find jobs that are right for them -- do things differently from the typical job seeker. Among other things, they are skilled at writing and distributing high impact resumes and letters that open the doors to job interviews, offers, and career advancement.

It is these writing and dissemination skills you, too, can learn. In just a few hours, you can be communicating some of the most important messages of your life. Once you learn to develop a proper *message* and use the right *channels* to get the attention of employers, you will have unlocked the secrets to clearly communicate your capabilities to employers who, in turn, will invite you to job interviews. Transferring this important skill to you is our central purpose in writing this book.

The following pages are designed to put you into the class of successful job seekers. If you follow the steps in this book, you should become an effective resume and letter writer. You will gain important knowledge and skills for opening doors which once seemed closed to you. Better still, luck will come your way as you become better prepared to take advantage of new opportunities in the job market.

A DIFFERENT APPROACH

Why produce another resume and letter writing book in an already crowded sea of such books? Simply because we have found few effective books on these subjects. We see a need for a different type of resume and letter writing book which would do 10 things not commonly found in other books:

1. It should be *comprehensive and complete*, including each step in the writing and distribution processes.

2. It should include *alternative methods* for creating different types of resumes and letters rather than offer only *"one best way"*.

3. It should be linked to the larger career planning and job search *process* as well as based upon the most advanced career development *methods*.

4. It should treat resume and letter writing as a *skill* that can be quickly learned and applied.

5. It should examine resume and letter writing and distribution as key *communication processes* requiring attention to the details of communication.

6. It should include *distribution skills* along with the more traditional writing skills.

7. It should deal with the *form, structure, content, and process* of writing and distributing resumes and letters.

8. It should incorporate *self-evaluation mechanisms* to be a truly self-directed guide.

9. It should include *examples* of effective resumes and letters, but these examples must be designed to illustrate important writing and distribution principles -- they are not to be creatively plagiarized.

10. It should be *easy-to-use and effective*, with a generous inclusion of self-directed exercises, illustrations, examples, and resources interspersed with a readable text.

Above all, you will find this is not another typical book on how to write *"job-winning"* resumes. Most such books present page after page of examples of supposedly outstanding resumes. Some even include cover letters, but only a few tell you what to do with your resume once you finish the writing exercise. Many implicitly or explicitly urge you to creatively plagiarize their pages of examples.

While easy to write and simple to follow, many of these traditional resume books do a disservice to both job seekers and employers. Quite frankly, they are a plague on the house of employers who must read hundreds of similar *"model"* products. For job seekers, these books are at best incomplete and at worst inaccurate; most are misleading. Imitated models simply are not the types of resumes and letters employers wish to receive. They want to know about the *"unique you"*. If you write high impact resumes and letters, you will communicate a refreshing *"unique you"* to employers.

Employers want to know about the "unique you". If you write high impact resumes and letters you will communicate a refreshing "unique you" to employers.

What we find most incomplete and misleading is a failure to relate resume and letter writing skills to the larger career planning and job search processes. For resume and letter writing is only one step among other equally important job search activities. These include:

1. identifying skills
2. specifying an objective
3. conducting research
4. networking for job leads
5. interviewing for jobs
6. negotiating salary and terms of employment

This book includes these other job search components in its examination of resumes and letters. In addition, the following pages are based upon years of successful experience with thousands of clients and in close collaboration with employers who read hundreds of resumes each year.

USES AND USERS

Given the self-directed format of this book, you can learn to effectively write and distribute resumes and letters at your own pace, without external guidance. At the same time, we designed this book for use in classrooms where career planning and job search methods are taught. It requires no skills other than what most people already possess -- the ability to learn, communicate, organize, analyze, and engage in new activities. If you want to achieve the maximum benefit from this book, you must demonstrate discipline, persistence, and creativity -- the same qualities important to conducting an effective job search.

Many individuals should find this book useful. We purposefully wrote this book for a general audience, but it also will assist individuals with specialized needs. If you are a high school graduate or a college student entering, re-entering, or advancing in the job market, this book will respond to your needs. It can be used productively by anyone regardless of age, educational background, occupation, or employment situation. Young and old -- new employees as well as retirees -- can use this book effectively. Given the strong process and data-base orientations of this book, page after page will respond to the job and career needs of engineers, lawyers, teachers, students, auto workers, civil servants, salespersons, secretaries, blacks, whites, males, females, and any other conceivable category of people. The inexperienced, underemployed, unemployed, and soon to be displaced will find this book especially helpful in facing an uncertain and disquieting, yet hopeful, future.

WHAT COMES NEXT

The remainder of the book is organized to be comprehensive, integrated, and easy-to-use. It begins with basic concepts, develops specific production steps and techniques, and ends with effective marketing and management strategies.

The next four chapters set the framework for writing resumes and letters. Chapter Three discusses 23 myths preventing individuals from effectively writing and distributing resumes and letters. These myths are challenged with corresponding realities for improving one's effectiveness in the job search. Chapter Four introduces the concept of the resume in relation to a dynamic seven-step career development process embedded in philosophy, ethics, and methods. Chapter Five focuses on important organizational principles. It explains the overall time frame for producing, targeting, and distributing the resume as well as outlines a hypothetical action plan for organizing your job search. Chapter Six examines alternative types of resumes and formats as well as outlines the internal structuring of resume elements, including the use of resume language.

Chapter Seven begins the actual production phase. This chapter takes you step-by-step through each section of the resume -- statement of objective, functional abilities and skills, education, experience, personal information, etc. It includes the necessary worksheets so you can generate the key information for each section.

Chapter Eight guides you through the process by pulling your resume together, evaluating it according to both internal and external criteria, and producing and distributing it for maximum impact. This chapter also gives you useful hints for producing high quality at low cost.

Chapter Nine is your letter writing chapter. Here you examine resume, cover, approach, and thank-you letters in terms of their purpose, structure, production, and distribution.

Chapter Ten is the critical action chapter. Here you examine the best marketing and management techniques for getting your resumes and letters in both the publicized and hidden job markets. We also include a record-keeping section to help you further reinforce and redirect your marketing strategies for maximum effect.

Chapter Eleven concludes with a discussion of anticipated results; the importance of further integrating the resume and letter writing phases into your overall job search campaign; and the need for persistence, discipline, and follow-through.

Chapter Twelve is your guide to other career planning and job search resources. Here we present a review of the literature with special attention on identifying the best quality resources for planning this and other stages of your job search. This chapter also includes a bibliography. The final section of the book includes a listing of key job search resources that can be conveniently ordered through Impact Publications. This is your career planning bookstore and library offering many titles that may be difficult to find in your local library and bookstore.

SUCCESS THROUGH IMPLEMENTATION

Resumes and letters are key communication *products* for promoting a larger job search *process*. You produce and distribute them in order to get job interviews which hopefully lead to job offers. If produced and marketed properly, resumes and letters have desired results. They especially work well for individuals who are committed to following-through with the step-by-step procedures outlined in this book.

The single most important reason many job seekers fail to achieve success is their inability to *implement and follow-through*. Understanding a process as well as knowing how to put good form and content into your resumes and letters are critical first steps for achieving success -- but they are not enough. Success comes to those who follow-through in practicing each step in the process. At the very least, this means sharpening your pencils, completing the exercises, drafting resumes and letters, evaluating the drafts, and distributing and managing the final product. This takes time and effort; it involves mundane mechanical activities as well as higher-level analytical, problem-solving activities.

Taking shortcuts is the
sure way to cut short your
job search effectiveness.

Taking shortcuts is the sure way to cut short your job search effectiveness! The benefits you will reap from this book are in direct proportion to the amount of time and work you devote to producing the final product. As is so often the case, there are no such things as free lunches, or quick and easy ways to job placement.

We wish you well in your job search and hope that you *implement* with gusto! In so doing, you may also experience what many of our students and clients report with increasing frequency -- greater self-confidence, self-esteem, career direction, and job satisfaction. Most importantly, they get *results* from their high impact resumes and letters. We're convinced the additional time and effort you devote to making your resumes and letters more effective are well worth the investment. At the very minimum, the quality of resumes and letters you produce reflects how you feel about yourself -- and employers.

Chapter Three

OVERCOME MYTHS
WITH NEW REALITIES

Numerous myths surround the production and distribution of resumes and job search letters. Unfortunately, many of these myths prevent individuals from becoming effective in today's job market. Indeed, many job seekers muddle-through the job market with questionable perceptions of how it works and what they should do to achieve maximum impact. Combining facts, stereotypes, myths, and folklore -- gained from a mixture of logic, experience, and advice from well-meaning friends and relatives -- these perceptions lead job seekers down several unproductive paths. Many of these myths are responsible for some of the major errors involved in writing and distributing written job search communication. Understanding these myths and corresponding realities, as well as how they relate to the larger job search, is the first step toward building effective resume and letter writing skills.

Over the years we have discovered 23 recurring myths and corresponding realities relating to resumes, letters, and the job search. Let's take a look at these myths and realities as we prepare for writing and distributing your written communication to potential employers. Examined individually, these myths and realities illustrate *key principles* to help guide you in writing and distributing your resume and letters. Taken together, they make up an important part of a larger American job search folklore which continues to guide -- but more often misguide -- many job hunters.

GETTING A JOB

MYTH 1:   *The best way to find a job is to respond to classi-fied ads, use employment agencies, submit applica-tions, and mail resumes and cover letters to per-sonnel offices.*

REALITY: Many people do get jobs by following such formal-ized application and recruitment procedures. How-ever, these are not the best ways to get the best jobs -- those offering good pay, advancement oppor-tunities, and an appropriate *"fit"* with one's abilities and goals. This approach makes two questionable assumptions about the structure of the job market and how you should relate to it. The first assump-tion deals with how the job market does or should operate:

> *Assumption #1:* There is an organized, coher-ent, and centralized job market *"out there"* where one can go to get information on avail-able job vacancies.

In reality no such market exists. It is a highly de-centralized, fragmented, and chaotic job market where job vacancy information is at best incomplete, skewed, and unrepresentative of available job oppor-tunities at any particular moment. Classified ads, agencies, and personnel offices tend to list low pay-ing yet highly competitive jobs. Most of the best jobs -- high level, excellent pay, least competitive -- are neither listed nor advertised; they are uncovered through word-of-mouth. When seeking employment, your most fruitful strategy will be to conduct re-search and informational interviews on what is called the *"hidden job market"*. The second assumption deals with how you should relate to this job market:

> *Assumption #2:* You should try to alter your goals and abilities so they will fit into existing vacancies rather than find a job directly related to your strengths.

This may be a formula for future job unhappiness. If you want to find a job fit for you rather than try to fit yourself into a job, you must use another job search strategy based upon a different set of assumptions regarding how you should relate your goals and abilities to the world of work.

Resumes and letters to do not get jobs; they advertise you for interviews.

MYTH 2: *A good resume and cover letter will get me a job.*

REALITY: Resumes and letters do not get jobs; they advertise you for interviews. Your resume and letters are marketing tools designed to communicate your qualifications to employers. From the perspective of employers, resumes and letters are used to screen candidates -- who are basically strangers to employers -- for interviews. Few people ever get hired on the basis of their resume and letters. In fact, over 95% of employers indicate they hire on the basis of a personal interview. If you believe your cleverly crafted resume and letters have some magical quality to land you a job, you may end up engaging in a whole series of useless -- and sometimes embarrassing -- resume and letter writing activities.

MYTH 3: *The candidate with the best education, skills, and experience will get the job.*

REALITY: Employers hire individuals for many different reasons. Education, skills, and experience -- major information categories appearing on your resume -- are only a few of several hiring criteria. Surprising to some candidates, these criteria may *not* be the most important in the eyes of many employers. If, for example, employers only hired on the basis of edu-education, skills, and experience, they would not need to interview candidates. Such static information is available in applications and resumes. Employers interview because they want to see a warm body -- how you look and interact with them and how you will fit into their organization. They can get other information from additional sources.

The most important reason for hiring you is that the employer "likes" you.

Indeed, the most important reason for hiring you is that the employer *"likes"* you. How *"likes"* is defined will vary from one employer and organization to another. In some cases the employer *"likes"* you because of your educational background, demonstrated skills, and experience. In other cases the employer *"likes"* you because of your style and personality as well as a gut feeling that you are the right person for the job. The employer will determine or confirm these feelings in the actual job interview. So be prepared in the interview to communicate a great deal of information about yourself other than what the employer may already know -- your education, skills, and experience.

MYTH   4:   *You can plan all you want, but getting a job is really a function of good luck.*

REALITY: Luck is a function of being in the right place at the right time to take advantage of opportunities that come your way. Therefore, the best way to have luck come your way is to plan to be in many different places at many different times. You can do this by putting together an excellent resume and marketing it within both the advertised and hidden job markets. If you are persistent in implementing your plans, luck may strike you many times.

Luck is a function of being in the right place at the right time to take advantage of opportunities that come your way.

PLANNING RESUME CONTENT

MYTH 5:   *The best type of resume is one that outlines employment history by job titles, responsibilities, and inclusive employment dates.*

REALITY: This is one type of resume which may or may not be good for you. It tends to be the traditional chronological or *"obituary"* resume. It's filled with historical *"what"* information -- what work you did, in what organizations, over what period of time. This type of resume may tell employers little about what it is you can do for them. You should choose a resume format that clearly communicates your major strengths -- not your history -- to employers in relation to your goals and skills as well as the employer's needs. Your choices include variations of the chronological, functional, and combination resumes -- each offering different advantages and disadvantages, depending on your goals.

> *You should choose a resume format*
> *that clearly communicates your*
> *strengths -- not your history --*
> *to employers.*

MYTH 6:   *It's unnecessary to put an objective on the resume.*

REALITY: What ties your resume together in communicating to employers what it is you both want and can do? An objective -- stated at the very top of your resume -- becomes the central focus from which all other elements in your resume should flow. The objective gives the resume organization and coherence. It tells employers exactly who you are in terms of your goals and skills. If properly stated, your objective will become the most powerful and effective statement on your resume. Without an objective, you force the employer to *"interpret"* your resume. He or she must analyze and synthesize the discreet elements in each of your categories and draw conclusions about your capabilities and goals which may or may not be valid. Therefore, it is to your advantage to control the flow and interpretation of your qualifications and capabilities by stating the objective. Most people opposed to stating an objective on a resume (1) do not understand the importance of integrating all elements in the resume around key goals and skills, (2) do not know how to develop a good employer-centered objective, or (3) are uninformed because they feel they have to change the objective for each employer -- an obvious confession they do not know what they really want to do. Developing a resume objective is not a difficult task. If nothing else, stating an objective on your resume is a thoughtful thing to do for the employer. And employers *"like"* thoughtful people!

An objective . . . becomes the central focus from which all other elements in your resume should flow.

MYTH: 7:   *Employers appreciate long resumes because they give them more complete information for screening candidates than short resumes.*

REALITY: Employers prefer receiving one or two page resumes. Longer resumes lose the interest and attention of readers. They usually lack a focus, are filled with extraneous information, need editing, and are oriented toward your past rather than the employer's future. If you know how to write high impact resumes, you can put all of your capabilities into a one to two page format. These resumes only include enough information to persuade employers to call you for an interview.

MYTH 8:   *It's okay to put salary expectations on a resume.*

REALITY: One of the worst things you can do is to mention salary on your resume. Remember, the purpose of your resume is to get an interview. Only during the interview -- and preferably toward the end -- should you discuss salary. And before you discuss salary, you want to demonstrate your *value* to employers as well as learn about the *worth* of the position. Only after you make your impression and gather information on the job, can you realistically talk about -- and negotiate -- salary. You can not do this if you prematurely mention salary on your resume.

MYTH 9:   *Contact information (name, address, phone number) should appear in the upper left-hand corner of your resume.*

REALITY: You can choose from a variety of resume formats which place the contact information in several different positions at the top of the resume. Choose the one that best complements the remaining layout and style of the resume.

MYTH 10:   *You should not include your hobbies or any personal statements on a resume.*

REALITY: In general this is true. However, there are exceptions which would challenge this rule as a myth. If you have a hobby or a personal statement that can strengthen your objective in relation to the employer's needs, do include it on your resume. For example, if a job calls for someone who is outgoing and energetic, you would not want to include a hobby or personal statement that indicates that you are a very private and sedentary person, such *"enjoy reading and writing"* or *"collect stamps"*. But *"enjoy organizing community fund drives"* and *"compete in the Boston Marathon"* might be very appropriate statements for your resume. Such statements further emphasize the *"unique you"* in relation to your capabilities, the requirements for the position, and the employer's needs.

MYTH 11: *You should list your references on the resume so the employer can check you out before calling you for an interview.*

REALITY: Never put your references on a resume. The closest you should ever get to mentioning names, addresses, and phone numbers -- other than your's -- is a simple statement appearing at the end of your resume: *"References available upon request"*. You want to control your references for the interview.

Never put your references on a resume . . . You want to control your references for the interview.

You should take a list of references appropriate for the position you will interview for with you to the interview. The interviewer may ask you for this list at the end of the interview. If you put references on your resume, the employer might call someone who has no idea you are applying for a particular job. The conversation could be embarrassing. As a simple courtesy, you need to alert your references ahead of time to the possibility that someone might call them concerning your application. At that point, you want to brief your reference on the position you seek, explaining why you feel you should be selected by focusing on your goals and strengths in relation to the position. Surprisely, though, few employers actually follow-through by contacting your references.

PRODUCING THE RESUME

MYTH 12:   *You should try to get as much as possible on each page of your resume.*

REALITY: Each page of your resume should be appealing to the eye. It should make an immediate favorable impression, be inviting and easy to read, and look professional. You achieve these qualities by using a variety of layout, type style, highlighting, and emphasizing techniques. When laying out each section of your resume, be sure to make generous use of white space. Bullet and underline items for emphasis. If you try to cram a great deal on each page, your resume will look cluttered and uninviting to the reader.

MYTH 13:   *You should have your resume typeset and professionally printed.*

REALITY: You may want to go to the expense of typesetting and printing, depending on your audience. However, it is not necessary for most positions. As long as your resume looks professional, how it is set or run is of secondary importance. In some cases a typeset resume may look too professional for the type of position you are applying for and thus may communicate that you had someone else do your resume. Many word processors and electronic typewriters produce good quality type, and many copy machines will give you original quality copies. If you use a word processor, make sure you use a letter quality or laser printer. Dot matrix printers and many near letter-quality printers do not produce professional copy. They look mass produced.

MYTH 14:   *The weight and color of the resume's paper and ink is unimportant to employers.*

REALITY: Weight and color of paper and ink do count, because they are the very first things the employer sees and feels when receiving your resume. They make an important initial impression. If your resume doesn't look and feel right during the first five seconds, the reader may not feel good about reading the contents of your resume. Make a good initial impression by selecting a good weight and color of paper. Your resume should have a substantive feel to the touch -- use nothing less than 20-pound paper which also has some texture. But don't go to extremes with a very heavy and rough textured paper.

Weight and color of paper and ink do count . . . They make an important initial impression.

Stay with conservative paper colors: white, off-white, ivory, light tan, or light grey. Your choice of ink colors should also be conservative -- black, navy, or dark brown. If, on the other hand, you are applying for a less conventional position, especially one in graphic design, fine arts, film, interior design, or advertising where creativity is encouraged on resumes, you may decide to go with some more daring paper and ink colors.

MYTH 15: *You should make at least 100 copies of your resume.*

REALITY: Make only as many as you need -- which may be only one. Since it is not necessary to have your resume professionally printed and since many copy machines produce excellent quality copies, you have the flexibility to produce as many as you need.

Your needs will be largely determined by your strategy for distributing your resume.

WRITING LETTERS

MYTH 16:   *A cover letter should always accompany a resume.*

REALITY: It depends on what you are trying to do with your resume. In some cases you may just want to write a short note at the top of your resume indicating *"I thought you might be interested in our mutual interests."* The conventional approach is to include a cover letter when mailing your resume in response to a vacancy announcement. On the other hand, when your resume is hand delivered to employers or left with receptionists, it may require no letter or note whatsoever.

Your letter should be the sizzle accompanying the sale.

MYTH 17:   *The cover letter should attempt to sell the employer on your qualifications.*

REALITY: The cover letter should command attention and nicely provide a cover for an enclosure -- your resume. This letter should be professional, polite, personable, and to the point. The letter affords you an opportunity to demonstrate your personality and writing skills in a letter format. Remember, your resume is supposed to sell the employer on you. Your letter should be the sizzle accompanying the sale. The letter should mention your interest in the position, highlight your major strengths in relation to the position, and ask the employer for an opportunity to interview for the position. Avoid repeating in this letter what the reader will find in your resume. Keep the letter well under one page in length.

MYTH 18: *You should close cover letters with the traditional "I look forward to hearing from you" closing.*

REALITY: Like ad copy, you should close your letter with a request for *action*. At this point *"looking"* or *"hoping"* for action from the employer is not enough. Take initiative by stating you will call the employer on a particular day to inquire about the possibility of scheduling an interview. Try, for example,

> *"I will call you Thursday morning concerning any questions we both may have and to arrange an interview if we deem it is appropriate at this time."*

While this statement may appear somewhat pushy or *"assertive"* on your part, which it is, it does result in action. And that is what you want. If you call and are told the employer is not interested in interviewing you, that's okay since you need not sit around waiting to be called. You can now move on to other more promising job leads. On the other hand, you might call and talk directly to the employer who will find you interesting enough to invite you to a face-to-face job interview. In either case, you get results which you ordinarily would not if you just waited.

MYTH 19: *Letters are not very important in a job search. The only letter you need to write is a formal cover letter.*

REALITY: Your letters actually may be more important than your resume. In fact, cover letters are only one of several types of letters you should write during your job search. The other letters are some of the best kept secrets of effective job seekers. They may become your most powerful marketing tools:

- Resume letters
- Approach letters
- Thank-you letters

---

*Your letters actually may be
more important than your resume.*

Different types of thank-you letters should be written on various job search occasions:

- Post interview
- After informational interview
- Responding to a rejection
- Withdrawing from consideration
- Accepting job offer
- Terminating employment

These are some of the most neglected yet most important forms of written communications in any job search. If you write these letters, your job search may take you much further than you expected!

DISTRIBUTING RESUMES AND LETTERS

MYTH 20:   *It is best to send out numerous resumes and letters to prospective employers in the hope that a few will invite you to an interview.*

REALITY: Yes, if you play the odds, someone might call you. In fact, if you shotgun resumes and letters to 1,000 employers, you may have two or three invite you to an interview. However, this shotgun approach is most appropriate for people who are in desperate need of a job or who don't know what they want to do. Their resumes and letters tend to communicate a *"give-me-a-job"* mentality. You should avoid this approach and concentrate on targeting your resume on particular organizations, employers, and positions that would best fit into your particular mix of skills and objectives.

This shotgun approach is most appropriate for people who are in desperate need of a job . . . You should avoid this approach and concentrate on targeting your resume.

This approach will require you to network for information and job leads. With this approach you will seldom send a resume and cover letter through the mail. Instead, you will write numerous approach and thank-you letters for the purpose of inviting yourself to interviews. Your resume never accompanies these letters.

MYTH 21: *You should present your resume at the very beginning of an informational interview.*

REALITY: Your resume should be presented at the very *end* of the informational interview. After all, the purpose of an informational interview is to get information, advice, and referrals. You are not asking for a job. If you present your resume at the beginning of such an interview, you give the impression that you are looking for a job. Near the end of the interview you want to ask the interviewer to review your resume and give you advice on how to strengthen it and to whom to send it.

Your resume should be presented at the very end of the informational interview.

MANAGING YOUR COMMUNICATION

MYTH 22:   *Once you have distributed your resumes and letters, there is little you can do other than wait to be called for an interview or receive a letter of rejection.*

REALITY: If you do nothing, you are likely to get nothing. There are many things you can do. First, you can write more letters to inquire about your application status. Second, you can telephone the employer for more information on when the interview and hiring decisions will take place. Third, you can telephone to request an interview at a mutually convenient time. The first approach will likely result in no response. The second approach will probably give you an inconclusive answer. The third approach will give you a *"yes"* or *"no"*. We prefer this approach.

MYTH 23: *The best way to follow-up on your application and resume is to write a letter of inquiry.*

REALITY: Employers are busy people who do not have a great deal of time to read all their mail, much less sit down to compose individualized letters. Use the telephone instead. It's much more efficient and effective. Most important of all, you should monitor your resumes and letters by keeping records and regularly following up on your job search initiatives. Be sure to keep good records of all correspondence by mail, conversations by telephone, and meetings. Keep a separate file or a 4 x 6 note card on each prospective employer. Record your contact information and dates for all employers on a master record sheet so you can quickly evaluate the present status of your contacts as well as use it as a handy reference.

If you do nothing, you are likely to get nothing.

Writing and distributing resumes and letters is a serious business. To do resumes and letters properly and with impact requires specific writing and distribution skills centered around clearly defined strategies for getting a job interview. The chapters that follow convert each of these myths and realities into a set of *action steps* for producing your own high impact resumes and letters. If you follow these chapters carefully, you will indeed write and distribute your own resume and letters with sufficient impact to get interviews that eventually lead to job offers for jobs you want.

Chapter Four

UNDERSTAND RESUMES, LETTERS, AND YOUR JOB SEARCH

KNOWLEDGE AND POWER

The old adage that *"knowledge is power"* is especially true when conducting a job search. But in and of itself, knowledge is neutral. When applied, it can cut two ways -- for positive or negative outcomes.

Not surprising, many job seekers write resumes and letters based upon a little knowledge and advice they receive from well-meaning friends, relatives, and acquaintances. Always willing to give advice, they tell you that *"You should put _____ on your resume." "Here's my resume -- why don't you use it as a model." "Try this letter -- I bet it will work for you, too." "If I were you, I'd send out 300 copies -- and be sure to have it printed on colored paper."* Or, *"Good luck -- I had to do that, too, a few years ago!"* With help like this, you would think you were making progress with your resume. After all, what are friends for?

When conducting a job search, friends may give you comfort and share bits and pieces of street-wise knowledge. But they seldom impart a *system* for making your job search as effective as it should and can be.

If, for example, your car had a flat tire, would you take it to McDonald's for service or would you push it through a carwash in the hope it would somehow revive? Of course not -- that would be stupid. But that's exactly what many job seekers do when they are faced with writing resumes and letters. They go to the wrong sources and apply faulty principles for making an important process work in their favor. No wonder the whole process looks like a big game of chance. Using such an approach, you have to believe that luck will come your way if you are to keep your sanity in persisting with your job search!

Often following bad advice, many job seekers confirm another old adage: *"A little knowledge can be a dangerous thing!"* Follow the advice of well-meaning yet uninformed friends, and you may find yourself taking a long, long journey down numerous deadend roads. As we will see shortly, writing and distributing resumes and letters is serious business involving important writing and marketing principles centered around specific goals. You can and should do much better than borrowing the *"expert"* knowledge and well-meaning advice of friends, relatives, and acquaintances.

Resumes are one of the most imitated, plagiarized, and misunderstood documents produced and used in today's job market.

MYSTICISM AND MISUNDERSTANDING

Resumes are one of the most imitated, plagiarized, and misunderstood documents produced and used in today's job market. For many job seekers, they are simple to create. Just stick a sheet of paper in your typewriter or printer, put your name and address near the top, and begin listing your vital statistics -- just like others do. All you need to do is change the names, titles, and dates. This shouldn't take you more than two hours to complete. And while you are at it, don't forget to do a cover letter. Once the resume and letter are finished, make hundreds of copies, get a list of names, type envelopes, stuff them, affix stamps, and send them out to prospective employers in the hope that someone will have a job for you. Next, wait for all the replies. Your biggest problem will probably be trying to select which employers' offer you should accept!

Congratulations on joining the wonderful, magical, and costly world of direct-mail! The Postal Service, envelope makers, and printers may love you -- but few employers enjoy receiving such junk mail. Most will appropriately file your resume and letter where it belongs -- in the garbage.

> *Few employers enjoy receiving*
> *such junk mail . . . The typical*
> *product is a deadly document*
> *fit for the trash.*

Faith and hope continue to guide many people who produce and distribute resumes in this manner. The typical product is a deadly document fit for the trash -- which is exactly where most resumes find a quick and final resting place with employers who are bombarded with hundreds of ineffective resumes and letters each week. Nonetheless, producing a resume in this manner is quick, easy, and *"personalized"*. It gives you a false sense of making progress in what is an inherently confusing and chaotic job market. It also communicates the wrong message to prospective employers: you lack goals, appear unfocused, and may be uninformed, unprofessional, naive, or just plain lazy. You're probably a loser!

Even more interesting is to probe why people write resumes. Not surprisingly, they write resumes because everyone else does and, after all, employers expect to receive them. So they send many resumes to many employers as if employers don't have enough resumes to fill their files. Others monitor classified ads and send cover letters and resumes to total strangers in anticipation of getting jobs through the mail. Still others just hold onto their resume in the hope of eventually using it to hook an ideal job.

For the individual who has never written or used a resume, writing a resume seems to be an unnatural act. It's a foreign, confusing, bewildering, and exasperating experience, shrouded in mysticism and mysterious movement toward different types of jobs one may or may not be interested in doing.

DOING BETTER

Assuming we can do better, let's take a little time to understand the job market, your goals, employers' needs, and effective strategies for penetrating today's job market. With a little bit of this knowledge, you will acquire power to affect positive job search outcomes. You will know exactly what you should be doing when writing and distributing resumes and letters. Acquiring this knowledge takes a few hours. It's a good investment of your time, because the results can be dramatic for both your self-esteem and job search effectiveness.

KNOW WHAT YOU ARE DOING, AND WHERE YOU ARE GOING

If not mysticism, resumes and letters are at least surrounded by plenty of myths, misunderstanding, misinformation, and wishful thinking. These are largely based upon one very simple problem -- the failure to understand what a resume is (*definition*) and what it is expected to do (*outcomes*). In other words, we must define a resume and examine its expected outcomes for both you and employers. In the simplest form, these are:

DEFINITION AND OUTCOMES

DEFINITION: A resume is an *advertisement* of who you are in terms of your competencies, accomplishments, and future capabilities. It is your chief marketing tool or calling card for opening the doors of prospective employers.

YOUR EXPECTED OUTCOMES: From the job applicant's perspective, resumes are supposed to help get *interviews* which, in turn, lead to job offers.

> | EMPLOYERS' | From the employers' perspective, resumes |
> | EXPECTED | are supposed to communicate *value*, i.e., |
> | OUTCOMES: | what applicants will do for them. In addi- |
> | | tion, resumes are mechanisms for *screening* |
> | | candidates for interviews. |

You should understand one other very important point about resumes from the perspective of employers who must read and react to them. Employers are not seeking to hire your history -- they want to know your capabilities in order to predict your future performance in their organization. Based upon a cursory reading of resumes and letters, they seek to screen a limited number of candidates. Screening simplifies what they want to do the most -- hire a capable individual, do it soon, and take as little time as possible from their busy schedule.

Employers are not seeking to hire your history -- they want to know your capabilities in order to predict your future performance in their organization.

When writing resumes and letters, always remember *your purpose*: you are *advertising yourself for an interview* -- and not for a job. Job offers only come *after* interviews. Effective resumes and letters should make prospective employers want to meet you in person to discuss your qualifications and possible contributions to their organization. These documents should clearly and factually communicate to employers what it is you can do *for them*. Most important, your resumes and letters should be honest, positive, concise, easy-to-read -- and *represent you and your major strengths*.

Knowing what resumes and letters are and what they are supposed to do makes their production and distribution both easy and time consuming. They are *easier* to write because you can develop resume and letter content around the purpose of these documents. They become *time consuming* to produce because you must write your own rather than imitate or plagiarize someone else's examples. You must begin from your own ground of experience in developing a resume and letters which clearly communicate:

- Who you are in terms of skills and capabilities.

- What you want to do in terms of your job and career goals.

- What you are most likely to do in the future for an employer.

Your resumes and letters should
be honest, positive, concise,
easy-to-read -- and represent you
and your major strengths.

Since you must project your *past and present* into the employer's *future*, such documents take time, effort, care, and professionalism on your part to produce and distribute. You can get advice from others, but you must produce resumes and letters by yourself based upon a thorough inventory of your past and present as well as projections into the future.

MULTI-FUNCTIONAL DOCUMENTS

Resumes and letters play several roles in the overall career planning and job search processes. While they advertise you for job interviews, a resume also performs other important communication functions relating to the larger job search process:

┌──────── **FUNCTIONS OF RESUMES** ────────┐

- Reviews your experience and communicates your potential value to employers.

- Provides information as part of your file in any placement service you use.

- Accompanies your application letters in response to vacancy announcements.

- Becomes an important element in the informational interview process.

- Focuses and communicates your job objective and qualifications around your major strengths.

- Serves as supplemental information to employment applications and letters of inquiry about possible job openings.

- Informs your personal and professional contacts -- friends, relatives, colleagues, alumni, former employers, etc. and those writing letters of recommendation and providing reference information for you -- about your job objective and qualifications.

You should keep these functions in mind as you develop each section of your resume and letters. They will help focus the content of your writing.

UNDERSTANDING THE CAREER DEVELOPMENT AND JOB SEARCH PROCESSES

Resumes and letters play a central role in the larger career development and job search processes. If you understand how resumes and letters relate to these processes, you will know how, when, and where to effectively target them for making the processes best work for you.

Career development is a process involving the movement from one set of career activities to another. In the most comprehensive and integrated form, this process involves four major steps, each with specific characteristics and activities. Our model of this process is diagrammed on page 43.

If you want to fully benefit from this process, you should develop a systematic plan of action. This plan consists of assessing your abilities, skills, motivations, and interests (*Stage 1*); exploring career alternatives and options (*State 2*); developing job search competencies (*Stage 3*); and

CAREER DEVELOPMENT PROCESS

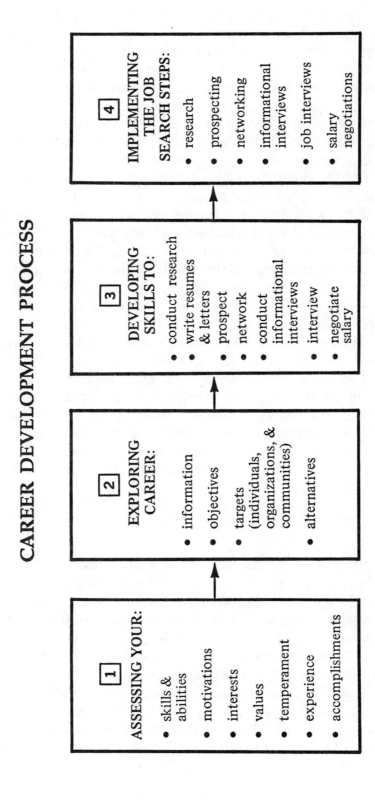

1 ASSESSING YOUR:
- skills & abilities
- motivations
- interests
- values
- temperament
- experience
- accomplishments

2 EXPLORING CAREER:
- information
- objectives
- targets (individuals, organizations, & communities)
- alternatives

3 DEVELOPING SKILLS TO:
- conduct research
- write resumes & letters
- prospect
- network
- conduct informational interviews
- interview
- negotiate salary

4 IMPLEMENTING THE JOB SEARCH STEPS:
- research
- prospecting
- networking
- informational interviews
- job interviews
- salary negotiations

using your newly acquired competencies and knowledge for getting a job and advancing your career (*Stage 4*).

Writing effective resumes and letters is an important job search competency within the career development stages. These written activities, in turn, are related to several other job search activities which are illustrated on page 45.

The *job search process* consists of seven separate yet closely related steps. And resume and letter writing lie at the very heart of this process (*Step 3*). As illustrated on page 45, these products should not be written in isolation of the other steps. For example, prior to writing your resume, you should know your abilities and skills (*Step 1*) and work objective (*Step 2*). At the same time, conducting research (*Step 4*) and prospecting, networking, and conducting informational interviews (*Step 5*) should come prior to, during, and after writing the resume. These are mutually reinforcing steps which provide useful feedback for improving the overall job search process. After completing these steps, you should be well prepared to interview and negotiate the job offer (*Step 6*) as well as start your new job or career (*Step 7*).

The following chapters relate Steps 1 and 2 of the job search process to developing effective resumes and letters. These steps consist of several self-directed exercises which clarify and specify your abilities and objectives as well as generate a comprehensive data-base for writing your resume. This is the subject of Chapter Seven. Steps 4 and 5 are important for refining your resume and for penetrating the informal or hidden job market. We discuss this specialized use of resumes for prospecting, networking, and conducting informational interviews in Chapter Ten.

APPROACH AND ETHICS

Our approach to resume and letter writing differs from many standard manuals on these subjects. Over-emphasizing *form*, many books neglect the important *substance* that needs to go into resumes and letters. They attempt to simplify resume and letter writing with numerous examples which you are encouraged to copy. Such an approach often results in ineffective resumes and letters which quickly find their way into employers' *"circular files"* -- wastepaper cans.

We, instead, use an inductive, contingency approach. This approach emphasizes the need to develop both form and substance in resumes and letters. Our approach also stresses the importance of relating resume and letter activities to the larger career development and job search processes.

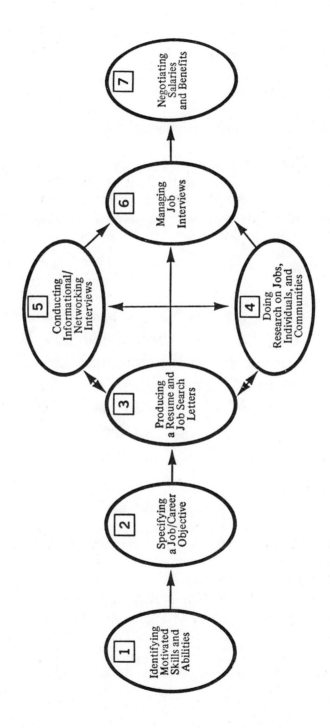

ACTIVITIES IN JOB SEARCH PROCESS

1 Identifying Motivated Skills and Abilities

2 Specifying a Job/Career Objective

3 Producing a Resume and Job Search Letters

4 Doing Research on Jobs, Individuals, and Communities

5 Conducting Informational/Networking Interviews

6 Managing Job Interviews

7 Negotiating Salaries and Benefits

Basic to this approach is the belief that resumes and letters should communicate:

- What you **want** to do.

- What you *can* do.

- What you *will* do for employers.

You can develop such resumes and letters by first creating a comprehensive data-base which outlines your abilities and experience in relation to your objective. If you use this data-base for developing each section of your resumes and letters, you will be able to communicate your *strengths* in relationship to employers' needs.

Using our approach, your resumes
and letters become unique,
personalized documents which
stand out from the crowd of
typical dull and copy-cat
resumes and letters.

Since employers' needs and expectations differ, so too should your resumes and letters. We see no *"one best"* resume and letter for all employers. Using our approach, your resumes and letters become unique, personalized documents which stand out from the crowd of typical dull and copy-cat resumes and letters.

Our approach also stresses a particular *ethical position*. Some people, after learning how to develop and use positive resume and letter language, get carried away and exaggerate facts. Hyping a resume or letter is deceptive and unethical. As with most advertising, a fine line exists between ethical and unethical sales techniques. However you decide to communicate your strengths to employers, it is essential that you always demonstrate your honesty, integrity, and forthrightness. We have yet to see any value in developing a rip-off mentality or becoming a con-artist in getting a job. You must be professional at all times in your job search, and especially in your written communication. You can do this by (1) generating the facts about your strengths (self-assessment) and (2) using positive language to communicate those facts to others.

Never create a situation that would raise a question about your honesty and integrity. If you do, you may be asked during the interview to explain what you *"hyped"* in your letter or resume. This could result in embarrassment as well as a different outcome than you intended -- a rejection.

---

*Be honest, but don't
be stupid!*

At the same time, honesty and forthrightness should not create new liabilities for you. Honest people sometimes say the dumbest things about themselves: they confess their negatives, undersell themselves, or fail to communicate their strengths. Being ethical doesn't mean you must talk about what is wrong with you. Our rule for job search ethics is simple: Be honest, but don't be stupid!

Chapter Five

ORGANIZE YOUR TIME AND ACTIVITIES

One of the most difficult tasks in any job search is organizing sufficient time to find a job. Each activity, be it self-assessment or writing a resume, takes hours of precious time. But time is not easy to find if you are already committed to other daily and weekly routines. If you work full-time, the problem of finding time becomes even more serious.

MAKE NEW TIME

Indeed, we and others consistently find one important reason for job search failure -- the inability of individuals to devote the necessary *time and effort* to each job search step. They get sound advice on how to make the process work for them, but they go off and cheat on their time. Instead of spending 30 hours on writing their resume, they cheat by spending only four hours. Instead, of making 15 new job contacts (networking) each week, they cheat by only making two.

These time cheaters often come back after a few frustrating weeks and complain the job search process and strategies don't work for them. Our nicest, nondirective responses:

*How many new job contacts did you **really** make this week? May I please see your networking records?*

*How many hours did you **really** spend putting this resume together? Let's see the data-base you generated.*

Guess what their responses are to these questions? Yes, they devoted a little time and a little effort in the hope they would get a big payoff. They thought they could short-cut the process. Not that they are lazy; they just didn't seriously manage their time. In fact, some even confess *"I'm so busy, I just don't have that much time. What can I do?"* Our sobering and more directive response:

Are you really serious about finding a job? What exactly are your priorities at this stage in your life? So far you haven't made enough time to do this properly. It looks as if your job search is not a priority. Am I right?

If finding a job is one of your priorities, then let's make it a priority by better using your time. Let's start over again. However, this time let's make some changes in your daily routines. First, examine your time. Second, reorganize and reserve sufficient time for each job search activity. Third, start over with the very first job search activity -- self-assessment. When you get to the resume stage, follow our step-by-step procedures for putting it together with impact. If you spend two to three hours each day completing these steps, you should be able to complete your resume within one week.

Let's speak the truth about the possibility of going nowhere with your job search: If you can't find enough time to do this right, don't come back and waste my time with rationalizations.

The first rule for conducting an effective job search is this: you must find the time to properly organize and implement each step of your job search. A second rule automatically follows: organize, organize, organize in the process of implementing each step. You can't organize and implement unless you set aside sufficient time to do so.

But how do you find more time when you don't have extra time? One of the best ways is to examine several *"tried and tested"* time management practices that work well for others. These practices will help you find new time to organize your resume and letter writing activities. More importantly, time management practices are designed to relate activities to goals within specific time frameworks -- a perfect methodology for your job search.

You must find the time to
properly organize and implement
each step of your job search . . .
Organize, organize, organize in
the process of implementing
each step.

While you can complete a resume in a few hours by copying examples, you should be able to produce a first-class resume on your own within a few days if you follow time management practices. If not, your job search may become confusing, frustrating, and ineffective.

BETTER MANAGE YOUR TIME

You can easily begin your job search from your office, filing cabinet, or desk drawer. Your immediate needs are paper, pens, a typewriter or word processor, envelopes, stamps, a telephone, index cards, file folders, a nearby library, access to a copy machine, and this book.

As you begin organizing your job search, you may wish to examine a few *"time management"* books to help you better use your time. Such classics as Alan Lakein's *How to Get Control of Your Time and Life* (New York: Signet, 1973), R. Alex MacKenzie's *The Time Trap* (New York: AMACOM, 1972), or Michael LeBoeuf's *Working Smart* (New York: Warner, 1979) are filled with practical time management advice. You will find numerous other time management books in your local library and bookstore delivering the same basic messages. Taken together, they stress the need to follow this checklist of time management practices:

——————— EFFECTIVE TIME ———————
MANAGEMENT PRACTICES

[ ] Evaluate how you normally use your time each day; identify time wasters; keep a *"time log"* to monitor your time patterns.

[ ] Set objectives and priorities.

[ ] Plan daily activities by listing and prioritizing things *"to do"*.

[ ] Create some flexibility in your daily schedule -- do not over-schedule.

[ ] Organize 2-3 hour blocks of time for concentrated work.

[ ] Avoid interruptions.

[ ] Organize your workspace.

[ ] Process your paperwork faster by responding to it immediately and according to priorities.

[ ] Learn to say *"no"* and to shut your door.

[ ] Do one thing at a time.

[ ] Improve your ability and speed to remember, comprehend, and read.

[ ] Continue to evaluate how you best use your time.

Time management follows a rational process involving the setting of goals and relating results-oriented activities to those goals. Four key questions help organize the steps in this process:

1. What are you trying to accomplish?

2. How are you organizing to achieve your goals?

3. What results are you achieving?

4. Have you evaluated your progress and with what outcomes?

Your most important time management goals should be to prioritize and reserve time for specific job search activities. Otherwise, such activities may get lost in the shuffle of daily personal and work routines or become victim to crisis management. Indeed, some time management experts estimate that most people waste 80 percent of their time on trivia, because they fail to organize, set goals, and prioritize their activities.

Before re-organizing your time, you should inventory how you use your time. You can do this by addressing the statements in the following exercise. Although some of these statements may not relate to your particular situation, complete those that do.

┌─YOUR TIME MANAGEMENT INVENTORY─┐

1. I have a written set of long, immediate, and
    short-range goals for myself (and my family).   Yes   No

2. I have a clear idea of what I will do today at
    work (if student, at school) and at home.   Yes   No

3. I have a clear idea of what I want to accomplish
    at work (or at school) this coming week and
    month.   Yes   No

4. I set priorities and follow-through on the most
    important tasks first.   Yes   No

5. I judge my success by the results I produce in
    relationship to my goals.   Yes   No

6. I use a daily, weekly, and monthly calendar for
    scheduling appointments and setting work targets. Yes   No

7. I delegate as much work as possible.   Yes   No

8. I get my subordinates to organize their time in relationship to mine.   Yes   No

9. I file only those things which are essential to my work. When in doubt, I throw it out.   Yes   No

10. I throw away junk mail.   Yes   No

11. My briefcase is uncluttered, including only essential materials; it serves as my office away from the office.   Yes   No

12. I minimize the number of meetings and concentrate on making decisions rather than discussing aimlessly.   Yes   No

13. I make frequent use of the telephone and face-to-face encounters rather than written communication.   Yes   No

14. I make minor decisions quickly.   Yes   No

15. I concentrate on accomplishing one thing at a time.   Yes   No

16. I handle each piece of paper once.   Yes   No

17. I answer most letters on the letter I receive   Yes   No

18. I set deadlines for myself and others and follow-through in meeting them.   Yes   No

19. I reserve time each week to plan.   Yes   No

20. My desk and work area are well organized and clear.   Yes   No

21. I know how to say *"no"* and do so.   Yes   No

22. I first skim books, articles, and other forms of written communication for ideas before reading further.   Yes   No

23. I monitor my time use during the day by asking myself *"How can I best use my time at present?"*   Yes   No

24. I live in the present -- mindful of the past and aware of the future -- and I deal with the present by getting things done that need to be done.   Yes   No

25. I maintain a time log to monitor the best use of my time.   Yes   No

26. I place a dollar value on my time and behave accordingly.   Yes   No

27. I -- not others -- control my time.   Yes   No

28. My briefcase includes items I can work on during spare time in waiting rooms, lines, airports, etc.   Yes   No

29. I keep my door shut when I'm working.   Yes   No

30. I regularly evaluate to what degree I am achieving my stated goals.   Yes   No

Effective time managers respond *"yes"* to most of these statements. If your *"no's"* out-number your *"yeses"*, you should seriously consider acquiring some useful time management practices.

One way to begin reorganizing your time is to analyze how you use time by keeping a detailed activities log. Develop a time log, beginning at 7am and ending at 11pm. Use our form on page 55 for this purpose. Carry this log with you. After analyzing the data for a week, you should begin improving your time use by completing the goal-setting exercise on page 56.

TIME MANAGEMENT LOG

Date: ——————

Starting Time	Ending Time	Total Minutes	Activity Type	Individuals/ Groups	Who Initiated	Results/Outcomes/ Notes
8:30	9:00	30	W	Self	S	Completed revisions on report
9:00	9:15	15	TP	Mr. Oats	O	Resolved problem with prepaid order
9:15	9:30	15	M	Ms. Siets	S	Planned meeting with department heads

CODES:

Activity Type: W = writing   TP = telephone   M = meeting   C = conference   P = planning   D = dictating   I = inspecting

Who Initiated: S = self   O = other

GOAL SETTING

Objective	Specific tasks	Why do it?	Completion date	Resources needed: time, personnel, materials, etc.

The final way to improve your time use is to keep a card in your pocket and on your desk which asks you:

> How can I better use my time at present?

After two weeks of new time management effort, respond again to our 30 time management statements. Continue to review these statements at the end of each week until your *"yeses"* overwhelm your *"no's"*!

---

*Your goal is to get a job
that is right for you.*

ORGANIZE YOUR CAMPAIGN

As you incorporate our job search activities into your daily time schedule, always keep in mind what you are trying to accomplish. Your goal is to get a job that is right for you. This requires organizing specific activities within a definite time period. Since the activities are closely related to each other, they must be internally organized in reference to your final goal. We suggest that you treat your job search campaign as if it were a $1,000,000 investment. In fact, your job search time and effort may well yield $1,000,000 or more in additional income over the next 20 years -- if you do it right.

Your major job search activities should include those identified as key steps in the job search:

─── KEY JOB SEARCH ACTIVITIES ───

1. Identifying abilities and skills -- your strengths.

2. Setting a job/career objective.

3. Writing a resume and job search letters.

4. Conducting research on individuals, organizations, and communities.

5. Prospecting, networking, and conducting informational interviews.

6. Interviewing for a specific position.

7. Negotiating the job offer.

These activities can be conducted on a full-time or part-time basis, depending on your goals and your time schedule. However, there are certain activities you should conduct regularly. These involve questioning, listening, evaluating, critiquing, adjusting, and thinking about what you are doing and where you are going (see the Job Search Process illustration on page 45). Many people tend to become too involved in the urgencies of daily living and thus neglect to stand back and *think* about what is important to them. This tendency toward tunnel-vision needs to be corrected with broader and more integrative thinking. Do reflective thinking by occasionally sitting down for an hour or two to *evaluate* your situation.

Depending on your personal situation, you may wish to initiate a one, three, six, or twelve-month job search campaign. Obviously, the shorter your campaign period, the more hours you must devote to each job search activity. In our model job search campaign on page 59, we illustrate what can and should happen in a job search conducted over a six-month period. Your monthly activities could be further divided into weekly and daily targets. We strongly suggest that you plan job activities in advance; set aside time each week, preferably each day, to accomplish specific tasks.

While most job searches should be completed -- i.e., result in accepting a job offer -- within three months, some are completed within one week; others may take as long as six months or more. We use the six-month period to illustrate the full range of activities and likely outcomes.

Remember, our model is hypothetical. While you may wish to vary the time organization of your job search, to get the desired outcomes you should engage in each of the job search activities outlined in our model. If you front-load your job search by devoting more time to such prelimin-

ORGANIZATION OF JOB SEARCH ACTIVITIES

Activity	Weeks 1 2 3 4 5 6 7 8 9 10 11 12 13 14 15 16 17 18 19 20 21 22 23 24
• Thinking, questioning, listening, evaluating, adjusting	
• Identifying abilities and skills	
• Setting objectives	
• Writing resume	
• Conducting research	
• Prospecting, referrals, networking	
• Interviewing	
• Negotiating job offers	

aries as self-assessment, research, and resume and letter writing as well as accelerate your networking activities, you can expect interviews and job offers to come much sooner than illustrated in our model.

One word of caution before you head off to organize your time and plan your job search. Please do not fall victim to *too much planning* by slavishly following such a detailed plan of action. Planning may make you feel rational, but it does not guarantee competence nor positive outcomes. Unfortunately, planning has one major down-side: it can blind you to that wonderful experience called *serendipity* -- chance occurrences that lead to unexpected opportunities and success. Indeed, planning is fine, but flexibility and receptivity to opportunities is even better. Being in the right place at the right time is even more important than planning.

Luck is where preparation
and opportunity meet.

Luck plays a role in the job search. Closely related to planning, luck is where preparation and opportunity meet. You get lucky when you plan.

Your most important planning goal should be to reserve specific time periods for activities related to your job search. In so doing, you designate the job search as a top priority activity and routinize it within your daily schedule. The tendency -- especially when you see no immediate results, such as a job interview and offer next week -- is to procrastinate by saying you can do this work tomorrow or next week. Your job search should have a central place in your overall time management scheme.

COMPLETING THE RESUME

You can complete your resume in two to three hours if you imitate our examples or those of others. However, we don't recommend this quick and easy method. Instead, do this task properly and with impact by incorporating the larger job search process into your writing activities. You should be able to complete an outstanding resume within a week if you devote two to three hours each day to developing the data-base and producing drafts of the resume, as we outline in Chapter Seven.

According to our time scheme for organizing the various job search activities (page 59), approximately three weeks are reserved for resume development. This, however, assumes that the resume is a direct by-product of the two previous job search activities -- identifying abilities and skills and setting objectives. Once you complete these activities, you should be able to produce your resume within one day.

Chapter Seven includes the necessary worksheets and self-directed exercises for generating your resume data-base. While these are designed to help you generate a large amount of quality data efficiently, you may want to conduct a more in-depth analysis using our seven-step job search plan. By doing this, you will take advantage of the most advanced and effective job search techniques available.

PRINCIPLES FOR SUCCESS

While we have no quick and easy formulas for success, we have found 20 principles for conducting a successful job search. These principles have proved effective for many job seekers; they should work well for you. Rather than being facts, truths, or scientific findings, these principles emerge from research, theory, experience, and common sense. They work best when taken on the basis of faith.

PRINCIPLES FOR JOB SEARCH SUCCESS

1. *You should work hard at finding a job:* Make this a daily endeavor and involve your family.

2. *You should not be discouraged with set-backs:* You are playing the odds, so expect disappointments and handle them in stride. You will have many *"no's"* before uncovering the one *"yes"* which is right for you.

3. *You should be patient and persevere:* Expect three months of hard work before you connect with the job that's right for you.

---

4. *You should be honest with yourself and others:* Honesty is always the best policy, but don't be naive and stupid by confessing your negatives and shortcomings to others.

5. *You should develop a positive attitude toward yourself:* Nobody wants to employ guilt-ridden people with inferiority complexes. Focus on your positive characteristics.

6. *You should associate with positive and successful people:* Finding a job largely depends on how well you relate to others. Avoid associating with negative and depressing people who complain and have a *"you-can't-do-it"* attitude. Run with winners who have a positive *"can-do"* outlook on life.

7. *You should set goals:* You should have a clear idea of what you want and where you are going. Without these, you will present a confusing and indecisive image to others. Set high goals that make you work hard.

8. *You should plan:* Convert your goals into action steps that are organized as short, intermediate, and long-range plans.

9. *You should get organized:* Translate your plans into activities, targets, names, addresses, telephone numbers, and materials. Develop an efficient and effective filing system and use a large calendar for setting time targets and recording appointments and useful information.

10. *You should be a good communicator:* Take stock of your oral, written, and nonverbal communication skills. How well do you communicate? Since most aspects of your job search involves communicating with others, and communication skills are one of the most sought-after skills, always present yourself well both verbally and nonverbally.

11. *You should be energetic and enthusiastic:* Employers are attracted to positive people. They don't like negative and depressing people who toil at their work. Generate enthusiasm both verbally and nonverbally. Check on your telephone voice -- it may be more unenthusiastic than your

voice in face-to-face situations.

12. *You should ask questions:* Your best information comes from asking questions. Learn to develop intelligent questions that are non-aggressive, polite, and interesting to others. But don't ask too many questions.

13. *You should be a good listener:* Being a good listener is often more important than being a good questioner and talker. Learn to improve your face-to-face listening behavior (nonverbal cues) as well as remember and use information gained from others -- if they need improving. Make others feel they enjoyed talking with you, i.e., you are one of the few people who actually *listen* to what they say.

14. *You should be polite, courteous, and thoughtful:* Treat gatekeepers, especially receptionists and secretaries, like human beings. Avoid being aggressive or too assertive. Try to be polite, courteous, and gracious. Your social graces are being observed. Remember to send thank-you letters -- a very thoughtful thing to do in a job search. Even if rejected, thank employers for the *"opportunity"* given to you. After all, they may later have additional opportunities, and they will remember you.

15. *You should be tactful:* Watch what you say to others about other people and your background. Don't be a gossip, back-stabber, or confessor.

16. *You should maintain a professional stance:* Be neat in what you do and wear, and speak with the confidence, authority and maturity of a professional.

17. *You should demonstrate your intelligence and competence:* Present yourself as someone who gets things done and achieves results -- a *producer*. Employers generally seek people who are bright, hard working, responsible, can communicate well, have positive personalities, maintain good interpersonal relations, are likeable, observe dress and social codes, take initiative, are talented, possess

expertise in particular areas, use good judgment, are cooperative, trustworthy, and loyal, generate confidence and credibility, and are conventional. In other words, they like people who can score in the *"excellent"* to *"outstanding"* categories of the annual performance evaluation. Many want God!

18. *You should not overdo your job search:* Don't engage in overkill and bore everyone with your *"job search"* stories. Achieve balance in everything you do. Occasionally take a few days off to do nothing related to your job search. Develop a system of incentives and rewards -- such as two non-job search days a week, if you accomplish targets A, B, C, and D.

19. *You should be open-minded and keep an eye open for "luck":* Too much planning can blind you to unexpected and fruitful opportunities. You should welcome serendipity. Learn to re-evaluate your goals and strategies. Seize new opportunities if they appear appropriate.

20. *You should evaluate your progress and adjust:* Take two hours once every two weeks and evaluate what you are doing and accomplishing. If necessary, tinker with your plans and reorganize your activities and priorities. Don't become too routinized and therefore kill creativity and innovation.

Above all, you should not assume you must follow every principle or piece of advice we and others give you. Develop a healthy sense of skepticism and initiative. Since individual circumstances and situations differ, you should modify, adapt, innovate, and experiment throughout your job search. Our guidelines and principles will help you channel your energies into fruitful directions.

WORKING WITH OTHERS

Writing a resume, like writing letters, basically is a pencil, paper, typewriter, and wordprocessor exercise -- relatively passive activities.

Other job search activities, such as networking and interviewing, mainly involve interacting with individuals on a face-to-face basis. Therefore, the guidelines for writing an effective resume will differ somewhat from the principles for conducting an effective job search.

A good resume can be completed in the solitude of one's office or study. Just complete the worksheets and self-directed exercises, write drafts, and type the final product. But remember, the resume ultimately plays an important role in the most critical interpersonal encounter with employers -- the interview.

Since individual circumstances and situations differ, you should modify, adapt, innovate, and experiment throughout your job search.

Because resumes have this important interpersonal dimension, we strongly urge you to *field test* your resume by talking to others about it and your job search. Involve your spouse, family, friends, or acquaintances. Why not, for instance, form a job search or resume writing group? Such a group should meet regularly to share information, pool resources, critique each other's progress, and provide support. By doing this, you should greatly improve your chances of finding a job. Indeed, according to some career counselors, you may cut your job search time in half if you join such a group. Through these activities you will also form lasting and rewarding personal relationships; lessen your frustrations by sharing them with others who understand; and find the job search process to be more enjoyable.

The support and encouragement you receive from others will keep your motivation and self-esteem high as well as help you handle the psychological bumps and bruises associated with the job search. By all means get out from behind your desk and typewriter and talk with people about your job search. If you ask them for advice, you'll be surprised how concerned and helpful they will be. In so doing, the quality of your resume and letters will improve accordingly!

Chapter Six

DECIDE ON FORM, CONTENT, AND ALTERNATIVE FORMATS

Writing a resume is more than just putting information about your work history on paper. Like any effective piece of advertising, your resume must have good form *and* content. It should look and read like good advertising copy or an effective press release — grab attention and motivate the reader to take action.

FORM AND CONTENT

You can create good advertising copy by paying particular attention to how well you combine both the form and content of your resume. While most writers concentrate only on the content of their resume (*"What should I include on it?"*), you must be equally concerned about its form (*"What type of resume should I write and how should it look?"*). Questions relating to specific categories of information to be included must be related to questions concerning resume type and appearance.

Our concern with form versus content is central to writing an effective resume. *Form* — how you communicate your message -- is the very first thing communicated to the reader. *Content* -- what you include in your message -- follows after the reader has been sufficiently motivated by the form to read your message.

Form is indeed important in communicating your message to employers. Consider the fact that many employers receive hundreds of resumes each week. Not surprisingly, some resumes receive less than 15 seconds of consideration while others may be read all the way through. Why the difference? Form is the first thing noticed by a potential reader. Depending on its quality, the form may or may not motivate the reader to explore the document further. Thus, the form of your resume should be pleasing to the eye and easy-to-read.

> *It should look and read like good advertising copy or an effective press release -- grab attention and motivate the reader to take action.*

One word of caution before you tackle form and content questions. While you should not neglect form, neither should you over-emphasize it at the expense of content. A resume may be strong in content but weak in form, and vice versa. For example, you may have 10 years of increasingly responsible management experience, but you will greatly weaken your application if your resume has an inappropriate format, stresses unrelated information categories, uses awkward language, presents information in a crowded and sloppy manner, and is produced on cheap quality paper. Indeed, poor resume presentation may communicate an unanticipated and disasterous message -- that you are an unprofessional and careless individual. On the other hand, your resume may be written in the most professionally looking manner, with strong headings and clear language, and be produced on high quality paper. But if it fails to communicate the substance of your objective, abilities, and experience, your resume demonstrates proper form but communicates little content.

Effective resumes successfully communicate *both* form and content. The remainder of this chapter deals with how to best communicate through resume form and structure. Chapter Seven continues this theme by examining how to develop and communicate content within the various forms.

IDEALS AND PITFALLS

Since resumes play many roles, no single resume format or style is *"the best"*. Resume formats are more or less effective, depending on your goals, style, and audience. Ideally, high impact resumes should:

```
┌──────────── POSITIVES OF ────────────┐
│          HIGH IMPACT RESUMES          │
│                                       │
│  • Immediately impress the reader.    │
│                                       │
│  • Be visually appealing and easy-to-read. │
│                                       │
│  • Be concise.                        │
│                                       │
│  • Indicate your career aspirations and goals. │
│                                       │
│  • Focus on the employer's needs.     │
│                                       │
│  • Communicate your job-related abilities -- not past or │
│    present job duties.                │
│                                       │
│  • Stress your productivity in terms of your potential │
│    for solving employers' problems.   │
│                                       │
│  • Communicate that you are a responsible and purposeful │
│    person who gets things done.       │
└───────────────────────────────────────┘
```

Employers try to quickly dispense with hundreds of resumes. In fact, we have timed employers at hiring conferences spending an average of 10 to 15 seconds reading each resume. Other observers report 30 to 40 seconds per resume as an average screening time.

Since most resumes do not catch the reader's interest, you should try to make your resume stand out from the rest. At the very least, you should avoid the resume pitfalls frequently identified by employers and placement specialists as ones that can effectively kill your chances of being further considered for a position:

MOST COMMON RESUME PITFALLS

- Too long, short, or condensed.

- Poor layout and physical appearance.

- Misspellings, bad grammar, and wordiness.

- Poor punctuation.

- Lengthy phrases, sentences, and paragraphs.

- Too slick, amateurish, and *"gimmicky"*.

- Too boastful or dishonest.

- Poorly typed and reproduced.

- Irrelevant information.

- Critical categories missing (i.e., Where's the objective?).

- Hard to understand or requires too much interpretation.

- Unexplained time gaps.

- Does not convey accomplishments.

- Text does not support objective.

- Unclear objective.

- Lacks credibility and content.

The majority of these pitfalls relate to the form rather than the substance of the resume. They further substantiate the importance of developing an effective resume format *before* dealing with questions of resume substance.

PREPARATION AND WRITING

You will develop your resume within a three-stage process: preparation, writing, and production. Equally important, each stage has a set of sound principles you can learn and apply. The preparation stage, for example, involves creating a solid data-base from which to initiate the writing stage. Unfortunately, wanting to go directly into the writing and production stages, most people neglect to devote sufficient time and effort to the preparation stage. A thorough preparation means conducting a comprehensive self-inventory based upon a complete review of your work history, education, and related experiences as well as a clear understanding of your accomplishments and skills. Chapter Seven is designed to help you generate this data-base.

You should write your own resume for one simple reason: the final product should reflect *your* goals, abilities, and style. Alternatively, for a minimum of $50, a commercial resume writing service will be happy to quickly produce a resume for you. However, these services tend to follow a standard format which may or may not incorporate your unique qualities and abilities. You will save money and retain quality control over your resume by doing it yourself. The process will be both enlightening and ultimately more effective. However, should you be unwilling or unable to do this yourself, at least use this book to shop around for a resume writing service that incorporates our principles of effective resume writing.

SELECTING FORMATS

You will find many books and guides on how to write effective resumes. We recommend consulting some of these for examples of different types of resumes and corresponding formats. But do so with a critical eye. The easiest thing to do is to copy someone else's work. Our strategy is different. We help you create your own by outlining useful strategies for developing and targeting your resume. Then, and only then, do we present examples to illustrate important resume writing principles.

You should write your resume based on a solid understanding of yourself as well as your audience. You do this by first analyzing yourself and your audience as you begin to link your aspirations to employers' needs. Remember, you are not writing the resume to your mother, spouse, yourself, or the newspaper obituary column.

There are many different types of resumes from which you can select an appropriate format to communicate your qualifications to employers. The most common types include:

- Chronological resume

- Functional resume

- Combination resume

- Resume letter

Each type and corresponding format has advantages and disadvantages, depending on your purpose and audience. We include examples of these resume types in Appendix A.

Chronological Resumes

The chronological resume seems to be everyone's favorite. It is the standard format used by a high percentage of resume writers today. The $50-plus resume writing services and the typical resume writing books, for example, most frequently use this format. It is the easiest type of resume to produce.

Chronological resumes also are known in some quarters as *"obituary resumes"*. In other words, if you died today and we looked at your chronological resume, your resume would be excellent copy for writing a standard three-inch column obituary about what you did in the past. Furthermore, some people feel this resume literally *"kills"* your chances of getting an interview -- particularly if you are changing careers -- because it locks you into your past as well as fails to communicate your strengths.

The typical chronological resume has several standard characteristics, many of which are its major weaknesses:

- Often lacks a job objective.

- Work experience usually is listed in reverse chronological order and explained as formal duties and responsibilities rather than in terms of abilities, skills, and accomplishments.

- Dates appear first, followed by job titles and the names and addresses of former employers.

- The basic emphasis is on compiling a work history rather than projecting one's capabilities into employers' futures. It says a lot about what you did in the past but little about what you can and will do in the future.

While chronological resumes are the easiest to write in this traditional form, they are the least exciting and effective resumes for individuals beginning professional careers or making career changes. They force readers to interpret candidates' backgrounds and qualifications. If, for example, you have little work experience, a chronological resume clearly communicates this fact to employers.

If you choose a chronological resume, try to minimize the amount of interpretation required by the reader. Control the interpretations yourself by including an objective, relating your experience to the objective, emphasizing major strengths, and using a more appropriate language to express your strengths in relationship to both your objective and employers' needs. For example, describe your job activities and talk in functional terms which highlight your transferable skills. Leave out extraneous information which usually clutters this type of resume, such as height, weight, hobbies, and references.

Chronological resumes have several advantages and disadvantages. While they are much maligned by *"expert"* resume writers today, they do have one major *advantage:* most employers are familiar with them and expect to receive them. Sending a functional or combination resume to a traditional employer may upset him or her because its uniqueness violates the traditional norm of chronology. After all, a chronological resume has one major advantage for employers: it helps them screen in and screen out applicants based upon job titles and work history. On the other hand, functional and combination resumes enable *you* to structure the thinking of your audience around your strengths. You take the initiative in interpreting your qualifications throughout the resume rather than force the prospective employer to draw conclusions about your future performance based upon a reading of historical information.

Chronological resumes have other advantages too. They are relatively easy to write. You can highlight simply and effectively stable employment history. Employers find these resumes useful outlines for discussing your past employment record during the interview.

The *disadvantages* of the chronological resume are particularly evident for individuals changing or entering careers. Employment gaps stand out sharply. The format may emphasize too many unrelated job experiences. Your strongest competencies are not emphasized to your advantage. Overall, this format does not provide the best presentation of your background and abilities if you are trying to enter a new occupation.

Chronological resumes . . . force readers to interpret candidates' backgrounds and qualifications . . . Try to minimize the amount of interpretation required by the reader.

Since the majority of job applicants use this format, you can make your chronological resume stand out from the rest by writing it well and designing it tastefully. You can do this by doing the following:

- Include a functional work objective.

- Write functional descriptions of your work experience immediately following your previous position titles and places of employment.

We illustrate these principles in the two contrasting chronological resume examples in Appendix A.

Functional Resumes

The functional resume tends to be the logical opposite of the chronological resume. De-emphasizing dates, positions, and responsibilities while emphasizing qualifications, skills, and related accomplishments, this resume begins with a functional job objective and organizes skills into functional categories. The functional resume is internally coherent because all elements focus on an objective and an audience. This resume essentially outlines abilities and transferable skills and tells employers what you will most likely do for them.

Functional resumes are especially useful for individuals lacking work experience or for those trying to enter a new occupation where they lack direct job-related experience. While this is one of the most difficult resumes to compose, it is much easier once you develop the data-base defining your objective, skills, and accomplishments as outlined in Chapter Seven.

Functional resumes do have certain weaknesses if not done properly. For example, this type of resume can communicate *"fluff"* if not expertly structured around concrete experience and a clear objective. Some writers have a tendency to make generous use of a functional language which appears *"canned"* and says little about the specifics employers look for in candidates. Rather than grabbing the attention of employers, some of these resumes may turn off employers because they appear cleverly designed to cover-over the lack of experience. Reading this type of resume, employers may ask *"where's the beef?"* Lacking content, these resumes may raise more questions than you want to answer. Therefore, your functional resume must be a delicate balance between the employer's need to know *"the details"* and your desire to motivate the employer to invite you to the interview where you will talk about *"the details"*. Nonetheless, a well-structured functional resume can be an outstanding document for presenting your skills.

Combination Resumes

The combination resume combines the best elements of the chronological and functional formats. Although similar to the functional resume in describing and explaining experience, this format includes a brief employment history section. For many individuals, this is the ideal type of resume -- bridging both the chronological and functional resume formats and language.

Combination resumes stress skills and competencies yet include names and dates. These resumes enable you to stress your qualifications in both chronological and functional terms as well as handle employment history easily. As such, this is a unique and complete resume for many employment situations.

These resumes have one major problem: they are usually difficult to write. In addition, their functional and chronological sections may overlap and create annoying redundancy.

The combination resume combines the best elements of the chronological and functional formats . . . This is a unique and complete resume for many employment situations.

Resume Letters

Resume letters should be used if a resume is not available or if a situation is not appropriate for sending a resume. When using this letter, your goal should be to communicate directly to a specific person in an organization your skills and qualifications. This letter should follow the same rules for writing a good resume: be concise, use action verbs, identify the needs of the employer, and show how your abilities and skills can meet the employer's needs.

KNOWING YOUR SITUATION

The format you choose should reflect your personal situation. Consider your qualifications, your objective, your work history, and the kind of employer you seek before you select a style. The functional and combination resumes are conceptually superior to chronological resumes -- especially if your audience understands the superior quality of such resumes and knows what type of person they want to hire. Therefore, you should try to learn as much as possible about your audience.

Functional and combination resumes can be very effective in getting interviews which result in job offers. These resumes communicate four important things about you that employers want to know:

1. What you *want to do* (your objective).

2. What you *have done* (your work history).

3. What you *can do* (your pattern of skills and accomplishments -- your strengths)

4. What you *will most likely do* in the future (best guess of your future performance based upon how you answered questions 1, 2, and 3)

Above all, these resumes address the *needs of employers*.

None of these resumes have inherent superiority -- only advantages and disadvantages.

But none of these resumes have inherent superiority -- only advantages and disadvantages for different audiences with varied expectations, likes, and dislikes. If, for example, you want to advance within a particular occupational area and have a strong job-related background, by all means use a chronological resume. Use functional language which will further strengthen the objective and work experience sections of this resume.

On the other hand, if you are changing careers, we recommend writing a combination resume which emphasizes functional categories more than chronological ones. In this situation, it is important to communicate your transferable skills. This resume best bridges the gap between traditional and functional thinking. It should satisfy all audiences without alienating any particular one.

Finally, if you are entering the workforce for the first time or re-entering it after a lengthy absence, the functional format may be best suited to your situation. This is especially true for students and homemakers who are starting in the job market without a history of formal job titles.

CRITERIA FOR SELECTING RESUME FORMATS

Resume Format	Your Goal/Experience Base
CHRONOLOGICAL	Advance within your present occupational area. Demonstrate strong job-related background.
COMBINATION	Changing careers but have substantial work experience directly or indirectly related to the occupational area.
FUNCTIONAL	Lack work experience in an occupational area, wish to change careers, or re-enter the job market after lengthy absence.
RESUME LETTER	Use at appropriate time as a substitute for the other resume formats.

Whichever format you choose, remember: *we* are not your audience; *we* will not be interviewing you; and *we* will not be offering you a job. You must use *your* own judgment based upon *your* information on *your* audience. If you are uncertain about which format to use, experiment with the chronological, functional, and combination styles to see which one best communicates your qualifications to employers.

ORGANIZATIONAL GUIDELINES

After choosing a format, you should be ready to organize pertinent information for producing an effective resume. Organization and production should follow four distinct steps:

1. Creating a Data-Base (Chapter Seven)

2. Producing a First Draft (Chapter Eight)

3. Critiquing and Evaluating (Chapter Nine)

4. Producing and Distributing (Chapter Ten)

As you develop your data-base in Chapter Seven for writing your first draft, you should keep in mind the following *general guidelines* for organizing your resume:

GUIDELINES FOR
ORGANIZING YOUR RESUME

FORMAT AND ORGANIZATION: Internal organization of your resume should include several items. The following are *recommended* for *all* resumes:

- Contact information: name, address, telephone number
- Objective
- Qualifications or functional experience
- Education background

In addition, you should consider including some of the following *optional* elements:

- Work history or professional experience
- Publications, presentations, and research
- Memberships and affiliations

- Personal data
- Reference section
- Personal summary statement
- Miscellaneous information: hobbies, licenses, special skills *supporting your objective*

A very effective resume would combine several recommended and optional elements within a one or two-page format. The format should be enticing to the reader's eyes. Avoid cluttering; provide ample spacing and margins so the reader does not strain. Knowing that our eyes tend to focus on the middle and move from left to right and up and down when reading, we suggest using the form on page 80. With this format you:

- Center your name, address, and telephone number at the top of the paper. Capitalize your name.
- Capitalize all headings and run them along the left side of the paper.
- Place all descriptive material to the right of the headings.

You should examine other formats. However, we believe this one is kindest to your audience, because it is easy to quickly follow and read.

LENGTH: We agree with most resume advisors that the one-page resume is the most appropriate. We prefer it because it focuses the reader's attention on a single field of vision. This is a definite asset considering the fact that many employers must review hundreds of resumes each week. Research clearly demonstrates that retention rates decrease as one's eyes move down the page and nearly vanish on a second

RESUME FORMAT

contact
information

headings

descriptive
material

or third page! At first the thought of writing a one-page resume may pose problems for you, especially if you think your resume should be a presentation of your life history. However, many executives with 25-years of experience, who are making $100,000 or more a year, manage to get all their major qualifications onto a one-page resume. If they can do it, so can you.

SEQUENCING OF ELEMENTS:
The sequence of elements will vary depending on the type of resume you decide to use. The *chronological resume*, for example, should have the following order of elements:

- Contact information
- Objective
- Work experience (or education, depending on your objective and audience)
- Education
- Optional personal statement

We recommend using the following order of elements for a *functional resume*:

- Contact information
- Objective
- Presentation of transferable skills supported by achievements (*"Areas of Effectiveness"*)
- Education
- Optional personal statement

The *combination resume* should include the following sequence of elements:

- Contact information
- Objective
- Presentation of transferable skills supported by achievements
- Brief outline of work history
- Education

• Optional personal statement

In each resume *always place the most important information first*. For example, if your work experience is your strongest qualification, place it immediately following the objective. However, if your education is most relevant, place it ahead of work experience.

DETAILS AND BALANCE: Lengthy, detailed descriptions are inappropriate on a resume. They become liabilities rather than assets. Readers prefer a writing style which uses short succinct statements that get to the point quickly. Be sure to emphasize specific areas of expertise beneficial to the employer. Keep each section neat, organized, and balanced.

ABBREVIATIONS: Do not use abbreviations except for your middle initial. Use full descriptions and spellings. Avoid the use of *"etc.", "i.e.", "e.g."*.

DOCUMEN-TATION: You should view each section of your resume as providing supports for your objective. Each section should document your supports.

CONSISTENCY: Format should be consistent, especially tense of verbs, order of information, and layout.

LANGUAGE: Use crisp, succinct, expressive, and direct language. Avoid poetic, bureaucratic, vernacular, and academic terms. For example, instead of stating your objective as:

"I would like to work with a consulting firm where I can develop new programs and utilize

my decision-making and system engineering experience. I hope to improve your organization's business profits."

Re-word the objective so it reads like this:

"An increasingly responsible research and development position, where proven decision-making and system engineering abilities will be used for improving productivity."

Use the first person, but do not refer to yourself as *"I"* or *"the author"*. Always use active verbs and parallel sentence structure. Avoid introductory and wind-up phrases like *"My duties included..."* or *"Position description reads as follows..."* Do not use jargon unless it is appropriate to the situation, for example, *"can program in Fortran and COBAL."*

APPEARANCE: Use various visual techniques to emphasize important aspects of your resume -- spacing, marginal descriptions, centered headlines, underlining, bold letters, different type sizes and styles, upper case letters. Develop an attractive, uncrowded format. Remember, less is often more when deciding what to include in your layout.

The exact structure of each information category within your resume will vary depending on your objective and choice of resume format. Chapter Seven examines each resume category and provides worksheets and exercises for developing the necessary data-base for writing your first draft. We have included these worksheets and exercises because you need to generate a large data-base so you will have enough information to develop each resume section. At the minimum, your data-base should include the following:

BASIC RESUME DATA-BASE

CONTACT INFORMATION: Full name, address (office and home), and telephone number.

CAREER OR JOB OBJECTIVE: A one sentence statement of what you intend to do for the employer. Immediately follows the contact information at the top of the resume.

EDUCATION: Degree(s), school(s), highlights, special training/courses.

WORK EXPERIENCE: Paid and non-paid experiences -- employment, internships, volunteer work.

MILITARY EXPERIENCE: Rank, service, assignments, achievements, demonstrated skills and abilities.

COMMUNITY INVOLVEMENT: Offices held, organizations, dates, contributions, projects, demonstrated skills.

PROFESSIONAL AFFILIATIONS: Memberships, offices held, projects, certifications, licenses.

SPECIAL SKILLS: Foreign languages, computers, special equipment, artistic talent, etc.

INTERESTS AND ACTIVITIES: Avocations, hobbies, and special interests which relate to your objective.

```
MISCELLANEOUS:  • Salary requirements
                • Extent of job-related travel acceptable
                • Are you willing to relocate? To where?
                • When can you be available to start work?
                • References: May present employer be con-
                  tacted for a reference?
                • Anything else you think is important
```

Selecting what should go on a resume also involves making judgments concerning what *not* to include. We find several items to be inappropriate for most resumes, although some of these will be included in your data-base:

——— ITEMS NOT TO ———
INCLUDE ON RESUME

PRESENT DATE: Include it in a cover letter, if necessary.

PICTURE: Provide only if it is essential for a job, such as in modeling or theatre.

RACE, RELIGION OR POLITICAL AFFILIATION: Include only if it is part of the main thrust of your resume or a bona-fide occupational qualification.

SALARY REQUIREMENTS: Salary usually is negotiable, but it should only arise at the end of the interview or during the job offer -- not prematurely on a resume.

REFERENCES: Always make your references available upon request. You want to control the selection of references as well as alert your references that you are applying for a specific position and that they may be contacted.

PERSONAL INFORMATION:	Height, weight, age, sex, marital status, health -- few, if any, of these characteristics strengthen or relate to your objective. Some may, for example, if you are a model or karate instructor.
ANY NEGATIVE INFORMATION:	Employment gaps, medical problems, criminal record, divorced, fired. There is absolutely no reason for you to volunteer potential negatives on your resume.

REMEMBER WHAT'S IMPORTANT

When deciding what to include in your resume, always remember these important writing guidelines for creating high impact communications:

1. Your resume is your personal *advertisement*.

2. The purpose of the resume is to get you an *interview*.

3. Take the offensive by developing a resume that *structures the reader's thinking* around your objective, qualifications, strengths, and projections of future performance.

4. Your resume should *generate positive thinking* rather than raise negative questions or confuse readers.

5. Your resume should *focus on your audience* and should communicate clearly what it is you can do for them.

6. Always be *honest* without being stupid. Stress your positives; never volunteer or confess your negatives.

If you keep these purposes and principles in mind, you should produce a resume as well as conduct a job search that is both purposeful and positive. Your resume should stand out above the crowd as you communicate your qualifications to employers with impact!

Chapter Seven

STRUCTURE RESUME CONTENT

So what are you planning to put on your resume. Should you include an objective? What about your references, hobbies, and salary expectations? Better still, what should you leave off? What are the sources for this information? How should each section be developed and related to other sections? Do you have a good plan for putting each section of your resume together? Let's find some good, practical answers to these questions by examining the structure of your resume.

Communicating your qualifications to employers via resumes and job search letters requires that you produce particular types of documents that will have impact on employers. Your resume should represent your best self. Your best self includes your strengths and achievements reformulated and targeted around your career goals. This document must communicate both your goals and strengths in direct relation to employers' needs. You do this through a process of self-discovery that flushes out (1) what you do well, (2) what you enjoy doing, and (3) what you plan to do for the employer. After doing this, you take this information and reformulate it so that it becomes the basis for structuring each section of your resume and letters.

CREATE A POWERFUL
DATA-BASE FOR ANALYSIS

Our approach to producing high impact resumes requires that you follow a four-step procedure:

1. Create a large data-base.

2. Distill the data-base into concise one or two-page resume drafts.

3. Evaluate each draft.

4. Revise the final draft for production.

You need to begin with the data-base so you will have sufficient information to complete each section of your resume. This step involves recalling and classifying your past into proper information categories. When generating your data-base, always go for volume. It's best to begin with more and selectively distill it to less. You can always select and condense information if you begin with a large enough pool of data.

The remaining three steps primarily involve your analytical and creative writing skills. You must analyze and synthesize the information in your data-base as well as distill it into short yet powerful sentences and paragraphs. This is the most challenging aspect of developing a high impact resume.

We've designed exercises and forms in this chapter to help you complete the first step. They will help sharpen your recall, analysis, synthesis, and creative writing skills. Chapter Eight organizes the data generated in this chapter for completing the remaining three resume production steps.

As you put together your resume, keep in mind that your resume is not your life history. It is supposed to communicate your purpose and abilities to others. It advertises your *future* -- not your past. At the same time, you must show how your past is relevant to your future performance.

SPECIFYING CONTACT INFORMATION

The first item appearing on your resume should be your contact information. Make it both attractive and functional. It always appears at the top of the resume, preferably centered, and includes the following information categories and writing rules:

—————— INFORMATION CATEGORIES AND ——————
WRITING RULES FOR YOUR
CONTACT INFORMATION

Information Category	*Writing Rules*
NAME:	State your full professional name. Avoid the coldness of abbreviations, such as *"I. T. Snell"*. Do not use more than one abbreviated initial. If you use titles such as Mr., Mrs., Ms., Dr., or Ph.D., you may appear pompous and distant. It is best to capitalize all letters in your name.
ADDRESS:	Use home mailing address. Do not forget to include your zip code. If you are at a temporary location, include both permanent and temporary addresses. The purpose of your address is to get the mail to you as quickly as possible -- and not to indicate where you are *"from"*.
TELEPHONE NUMBER:	List telephone numbers where you can be reached during the day and evening or a number where a message can be left for you. The long distance area code should be included. If you are highly mobile, enlist a telephone answering service or buy a telephone answering machine. Be sure you record a

answering machine. Be sure you record a professional message -- a humorous message may not be appreciated.

FORMATS: Your contact information can appear in several alternative forms. Take for example, the following resume headings -- all of which are acceptable:

JOHN C. TALBORT

2261 Gateway Dr.   Richmond, VA 23612   823/467-9042

JOHN C. TALBORT
823/467-9042
423-467-2148

2261 Gateway Drive   Richmond, Virginia 23612

JOHN C. TALBORT

2261 Gateway Drive
Richmond, Virgnia 23612

823/467-9042
823/467-2148

JOHN C. TALBORT

2261 Gateway Dr.   Richmond, Virginia 23612   823/467-9042

JOHN C. TALBORT

2261 Gateway Drive   823/467-9042
Richmond, Virginia 23512   823/467-2148

JOHN C. TALBORT

2261 Gateway Drive   Richmond, Virgnia 23612   823/467-9042

Make sure your contact information is uncluttered and pleasing to the eye. Since it will be the very first piece of information the reader sees on your resume, it should invite one to read further.

STATING AN OBJECTIVE

The job objective normally appears immediately following your contact information. While some people consider this to be an unnecessary, pretentious, and optional item, we see it as necessary, professional, and thoughtful.

You have two options here: (1) place an objective on the resume, or (2) leave it off, but include it in your accompanying cover letter. If you put it in your cover letter, you won't have to re-type your resume every time you want to target your objective for a particular position. This is especially prudent if you plan to have your resume professionally printed. Use your own judgment.

The objective should be the central focal point to which all other elements in the resume relate.

We still prefer the objective at the top of the resume, because it should be the central focal point to which all other elements in the resume relate. If you know what you want to do and can state your objective in general terms, it can be used repeatedly for different positions and audiences.

The relative impact of these different strategies may be the old preverbial *"Six one way, half a dozen another"*. It may not make much difference in the end. But be sure you communicate, in some manner, your career direction. Otherwise, you may conduct a traditionally disorganized search with a weak chronological resume.

Using Objectives

Your objective should be a concise statement of what you want to do and what you have to offer to an employer. The position you seek is *"what you want to do"*; your qualifications are *"what you have to offer"*. Your objective should state your strongest qualifications for meeting employer's needs. It should communicate what you have to offer an employer without emphasizing what you expect the employer to do for you. In other words, your objective should be *work-centered*, not self-centered; it should not contain trite terms which emphasize what you want, such as give me a(n) *"opportunity for advancement"*, *"position working with people"*, *"progressive company"*, or *"creative position"*. Such terms are viewed as *"canned"* resume language which say little of value about you. Above all, your objective should reflect your honesty and integrity; it should not be *"hyped"*.

Identifying what it is you want to do can be one of the most difficult job search tasks. Indeed, most job hunters lack clear objectives. Many engage in a random, and somewhat mindless, search for jobs by identifying available job opportunities and then adjusting their skills and objectives to *"fit"* specific job openings. While you will get a job using this approach, you may be misplaced and unhappy with what you find. You will fit into a job rather than find a job that is fit for you.

Knowing what you want to do can have numerous benefits. First, you define the job market rather than let it define you. The inherent fragmentation and chaos of the job market should be advantageous for you because it enables you to systematically organize job opportunities around your specific objectives and skills. Second, since your resume will focus on an objective, you will communicate professionalism to prospective employers. They will receive a precise indication of your interests, qualifications, and purposes, which places you ahead of most other applicants. Third, being purposeful means being able to communicate to employers what you want to do. Employers are not interested in hiring indecisive and confused individuals. They want to know what it is you can do for them. With a clear objective, based upon a thorough understanding of your abilities, skills, and interests, you can take control of the situation, generate and demonstrate your value to employers.

Finally, few employers really know what they want in a candidate. Like most job seekers, employers lack clear employment objectives and knowledge about how the job market operates. Thus, if you know what you want and can help the employer define his or her *"needs"* as your objective, you will have achieved a tremendously advantageous position in the job market.

Transferable Skills

The first step in developing your objective is to understand your transferable skills. Transferable skills are skills which can be used in different job settings. Most people possess hundreds of such skills. Once you become aware of them, you will be better able to use a functional skills vocabulary throughout your resume.

Take, for example, the case of educators seeking career changes. While educators tend to view their qualifications as mastery of specific disciplines and subject matters, they also possess functional skills which are transferable to jobs and careers in business, industry and government. These skills first develop in childhood and subsequently expand through other life experiences, such as schools, universities, and community organizations. In the case of graduate students in the humanities, studies show that the most important transferable skills acquired in graduate training, in order of importance, are:

1. critical thinking	7. general knowledge
2. research techniques	8. cultural perspective
3. perseverance	9. teaching ability
4. self-discipline	10. self-confidence
5. insight	11. imagination
6. writing	12. leadership ability

Educators possess many of these and other transferable skills acquired while performing the role of educator. Teaching, for example, involves skills other than instructing:

___ organizing	___ problem solving	___ coordinating
___ making decisions	___ public speaking	___ managing
___ counseling	___ advising	___ reporting
___ motivating	___ coaching	___ administering
___ leading	___ evaluating	___ persuading
___ selling	___ training	___ encouraging
___ assessing	___ supervising	___ improving

Research and publication activities of academicians involve many additional transferable skills:

___ initiating	___ interpreting	___ analyzing
___ updating	___ planning	___ designing
___ communicating	___ estimating	___ implementing
___ performing	___ achieving	___ reviewing
___ attaining	___ negotiating	___ maintaining responsibility

Interacting with students, faculty, administrators, and staff requires using several skill-related personality qualities:

___ dynamic   ___ unique   ___ challenging
___ imaginative   ___ versatile   ___ sophisticated
___ innovative   ___ responsible   ___ diplomatic
___ perceptive   ___ concerned   ___ discrete
___ outstanding   ___ successful   ___ creative
___ tactful   ___ easy-going   ___ effective
___ reliable   ___ humanistic   ___ adept
___ vigorous   ___ competent   ___ efficient
___ sensitive   ___ warm   ___ aware
___ accurate   ___ objective   ___ honest
___ trained   ___ broad   ___ self-starter
___ expert   ___ outgoing   ___ strong
___ astute   ___ experienced   ___ talented
___ calm   ___ democratic   ___ empathic

Such transferrable skills are generic to other occupational areas. You may wish to identify and prioritize those which relate to your experiences. In addition, most individuals are capable of working with different types of objects and publics which are related to transferable skills:

___ data   ___ reports   ___ designs
___ recommendations   ___ systems   ___ unusual
___ inefficiencies   ___ programs   conditions
___ facts   ___ conclusions   ___ communications
___ feelings   ___ groups   systems
___ procedures   ___ art   ___ research
___ techniques   ___ methods   projects
___ project planning   ___ objectives   ___ approaches
___ relations   ___ individuals   ___ presentations
___ events   ___ information   problems
___ goals   ___ theories   statistical
___ processes   ___ records   analyses
___ statistics   ___ handbooks   ___ human
___ equipment   ___ inputs   resources
___ living things   ___ investigations   ___ costs
___ tools   ___ outputs   ___ duties
___ charts   ___ surveys   ___ plants
___ points of view   ___ strategy   ___ surveys
___ prima donnas   ___ growth   ___ energy
___ training programs ___ journals   ___ senior
                                                    executives

Identifying your transferable skills may be simple or complex, depending on how much time and effort you wish to invest. Career counselors have developed numerous inductive approaches -- mostly self-directed exercises -- for helping you identify your skills. Since you may want options, we outline alternative *"skills"* approaches, point out their strengths and weaknesses, and explain the importance of using redundancy to your benefit. We advise you to try several approaches and assess which ones give you the most useful information.

Intensive Skills Identification

Intensive Skills Identification is widely used by career counselors. This technique helps you identify which skills you *enjoy* using. Since you will need six to eight hours to properly complete this exercise, divide your time into two or three work sessions. The exercise consists of six steps:

1. *Identify 15-20 achievements.* These consist of anything you enjoyed doing, believe you did well, and felt a sense of satisfaction, pride, or accomplishment in doing. You can see yourself performing at your best and enjoying your experiences when you analyze your achievements. This information reveals your motivations since it deals entirely with your voluntary behavior. In addition, it identifies what is right with you by focusing on your positives and strengths. Identify achievements throughout your life, beginning with your childhood. Your achievements should relate to specific experiences -- not general ones -- and may be drawn from work, leisure, education, military, or home life. Put each achievement at the top of a separate sheet of paper. For example, your achievements might appear as follows:

SAMPLE ACHIEVEMENT STATEMENTS

"When I was 10 years old, I started a small paper route and built it up to the largest in my district."

"I started playing chess in ninth grade and earned the right to

play first board on my high school chess team in my junior year."

_____

"Learned to play the piano and often played for church services while in high school."

_____

"Designed and constructed a dress for a 4-H demonstration project."

_____

"Although I was small compared to other guys, I made the first string on my high school football team."

_____

"I graduated from high school with honors even though I was very active in school clubs and had to work part-time."

_____

"I was the first in my family to go to college and one of the few from my high school. Worked part-time and summers. A real struggle, but I made it."

_____

"Earned an 'A' grade on my senior psychology project from a real tough professor."

_____

"Finished my master's degree while working full-time and attending to my family responsibilities."

_____

"Proposed a chef's course for junior high boys. Got it approved. Developed it into a very popular elective."

_____

"Designed the plans for our house and had it constructed within budget."

2. *Prioritize your seven most significant achievements.*

```
┌──────── YOUR MOST SIGNIFICANT ────────┐
│               ACHIEVEMENTS            │
│                                       │
│   1. _____│
│                                       │
│   2. _____│
│                                       │
│   3. _____│
│                                       │
│   4. _____│
│                                       │
│   5. _____│
│                                       │
│   6. _____│
│                                       │
│   7. _____│
│                                       │
└───────────────────────────────────────┘
```

3. *Write a full page on each of your prioritized achievements.* You should describe:

- How you intitially became involved.
- The details of *what you did* and *how you did it.*
- What was especially enjoyable or satisfying to you.

Use copies of *"Detailing Your Achievements"* form on page 100 to outline your achievements.

4. *Elaborate on your achievements.* Have one or two other people interview you. For each achievement have them note on a separate sheet of paper any terms used to reveal your skills, abilities, and personal qualities. To elaborate details, the interviewer(s) may ask:

DETAILING YOUR ACHIEVEMENTS

ACHIEVEMENT # __: _____

_____

1. How did I initially become involved? _____
   _____
   _____
   _____

2. What did I do? _____
   _____
   _____
   _____
   _____
   _____

3. How did I do it? _____
   _____
   _____
   _____
   _____

4. What was especially enjoyable about doing it? _____
   _____
   _____
   _____

- What was involved in the achievement?
- What was your part?
- What did you actually do?
- How did you go about that?

Clarify any vague areas by providing an example or illustration of what you actually did. This interview should clarify the details of your activities by asking only *"what"* and *"how"* questions. Reproduce the *"Strength Identification Interview"* form on page 102 to guide you through this interview.

5. *Identify patterns by examining the interviewer's notes.* Together identify the recurring skills, abilities, and personal qualities *demonstrated* in your achievements. Search for patterns. Your skills pattern should be clear at this point; you should feel comfortable with it. If you have questions, review the data. If you disagree with a conclusion, disregard it. The results must accurately and honestly reflect how you operate.

6. *Synthesize the information by clustering similar skills into categories.* For example, your skills might be grouped in the following manner:

──── SYNTHESIZED SKILL CLUSTERS ────

Investigate/Survey/Read Inquire/Probe/Question	Teach/Train/Drill Perform/Show/Demonstrate
Learn/Memorize/Practice Evaluate/Appraise/Assess Compare	Construct/Assemble/Put Together
	Organize/Structure/Provide definition/Plan/Chart course Strategize/Coordinate
Influence/Involve/Get participation/Publicize Promote	Create/Design/Adapt/Modify

STRENGTH IDENTIFICATION
INTERVIEW

Interviewee _____   Interviewer _____

INSTRUCTIONS: For each achievement experience, identify the *skills* and abilities which the achiever actually demonstrated. To obtain details of the experience, ask *what* was involved with the achievement and *how* the individual made the achievement happen. Avoid *"why"* questions which tend to mislead. Ask for examples or illustrations.

Achievement # ___   Achievement # ___   Achievement # ___

Recurring Skills and Abilities:

This exercise yields a relatively comprehensive inventory of your skills. The information will better enable you to use a *skills vocabulary* when identifying your objective, writing your resume and letters, and interviewing. Your self-confidence and self-esteem should increase accordingly.

Checklist Method

One of the most popular approaches to skills identification is Richard Bolles' *"Quick Job Hunting Map"*. It is found in his book, **What Color Is Your Parachute?**, or it can be purchased as a separate workbook in both beginning and advanced versions (Ten Speed Press, Berkeley, CA).

The *"Map"* contains a comprehensive skills checklist for helping you build your skills vocabulary. You simply identify your most satisfying accomplishments, jobs, or roles in life and relate these to a listing of skills. Depending on how thorough and detailed you treat each experience, this exercise may take six hours to complete. The *"Map"* is easy to use and it yields an enormous amount of inter-related information on things you both do well and enjoy doing. The exercise gives you a fairly comprehensive snapshot of your past skill and patterns.

Other Alternatives

Alternative techniques are available for identifying transferable skills. Most are inductive self-directed exercises which identify skills based upon past experiences. Any of the following exercises can be used interchangeably to inventory your skills:

1. Write your autobiography with special emphasis on your pleasures and accomplishments. This may run from 30 to 200 pages or more. Analyze this document by identifying those things you most enjoyed doing and wish to continue doing in the future. Identify which skills cluster with your favorite experiences.

2. List all your hobbies and analyze what you do in each, which ones you like the most, what skills you use, and your accomplishments.

3. Complete John Holland's *"The Self-Directed Search"*. It is found in his book, **Making Vocational Choices: A Theory of Careers.**

4. Conduct a job analysis by writing about your past jobs and identifying which skills you used in each job. Cluster the skills into related categories and prioritize them according to your preferences.

Benefiting From Redundancy

The self-directed *"skills"* exercises generate similar information. They identify transferable skills you already possess. While aptitude and achievement tests may yield similar information, the self-directed exercises have three major advantages over the standardized tests: less expensive, self-monitored and evaluated, and measure motivation *and* ability.

Completing each exercise demands a different investment of your time. Writing your life history and completing the Intensive Skills Identification exercise as well as Bolles' *"Map"* are the most time consuming. On the other hand, Holland's self-directed search can be completed in a few minutes. But the more time you invest with each technique, the more useful information you will generate. We recommend creating redundancy by using two or three different techniques. This will help reinforce and confirm the validity of your observations and interpretations. If you are making a mid-career change and/or have a considerable amount of experience, we recommend using the more thorough exercises. The more you put into these techniques and exercises, the more your resume and other stages of the job search will benefit.

Understanding and Realism

Your objective should communicate that you are a *purposeful individual who achieves results*. It can be stated over different time periods as well as at various levels of abstraction and specificity. You can identify short, intermediate, and long-range objectives and very general to very specific objectives. Whatever the case, it is best to know your prospective audience before deciding on the type of objective. Your objective should reflect your career interests as well as employers' needs.

Objectives also should be *realistic*. You may want to become President of the United States or solve all the world's problems. However, these objectives are probably unrealistic. While they may represent your ideals and fantasies, you need to be more realistic in terms of what you can personally accomplish in the immediate future. What, for example, are you prepared to deliver to prospective employers over the next few months? While it is good to set challenging objectives, you can overdo it.

Refine your objective by thinking about the next major step or two you would like to make in your career advancement -- not some grandiose leap outside reality!

Projecting Into the Future

Even after identifying your abilities and skills, specifying an obejctive can be the most difficult and tedious step in the job search process; it can stall the resume writing process indefinitely. This simple one-sentence, 25-word statement can take days or weeks to formulate and clearly define. Yet, it must be specified prior to writing the resume and engaging in other job search steps. An objective gives meaning and direction to all other activities.

Your objective should communicate that you are a purposeful individual who achieves results. It gives meaning and direction to all other activities.

Your objective should be viewed as a function of several influences. Since you want to build upon your strengths and you want to be realistic, your abilities and skills will play a central role in formulating your work objective. At the same time, you do not want your objective to become a function solely of your past accomplishments and skills. You may be very skilled in certain areas, but you may not want to use these skills in the future. As a result, your values and interests filter which skills you will or will not incorporate into your work objective.

Overcoming the problem of historical determinism -- your future merely reflecting your past -- requires incorporating additional components into defining your objective. One of the most important is your ideals, fantasies, or dreams. Everyone engages in these, and sometimes they come true. Your ideals, fantasies, or dreams may include making $1,000,000 by age 45; owning a Mercedes-Benz and a Porshe; taking trips to Rio, Hong Kong, and Rome; owning your own business; developing financial independence; writing a best-selling novel; solving major social problems; or winning the Nobel Peace Prize. If your fantasies require more money than you are now making, you will need to incorporate monetary considerations into your work objective.

You can develop realistic objectives many different ways. We don't claim to have a new or magical formula, only one which has worked for many individuals. We assume you are capable of making intelligent career decisions if given sufficient data. Using redundancy once again, our approach is designed to provide you with sufficient corroborating data from several sources and perspectives so that you can make preliminary decisions. If you follow our steps in setting a realistic objective, you should be able to give your job search clear direction and create a well-integrated resume.

Four major steps are involved in developing a work objective. Each step can be implemented in a variety of ways:

STEP 1: *Develop or obtain basic data on your functional/transferable skills, which we discussed earlier in this chapter.*

STEP 2: *Acquire corroborating data about yourself from others, tests, and yourself. Several resources are available for this purpose:*

   A. *From others:* Ask three to five individuals who know you well to evaluate you according to the questions in the *"Strength Evaluation"* form on page 108. Explain to these people that you believe their candid appraisal will help you gain a better understanding of your strengths and weaknesses from the perspectives of others. Make copies of this form and ask your evaluators to complete and return it to a designated third party who will share the information -- but not the respondent's name -- with you.

   B. *From vocational tests:* Although we prefer self-generated data, vocationally-oriented tests can help clarify, confirm, and translate your understanding of yourself into occupational directions. If you decide to use vocational tests, contact a professional career counselor who can administer and interpret the tests. We recommend several of the following tests:

```
┌──────────── STRENGTH EVALUATION ────────────┐
│                                              │
│  TO: _____            │
│                                              │
│  FROM: _____            │
│                                              │
│     I am going through a career assessment process and thought │
│  you would be an appropriate person to ask for assistance. Would │
│  you please candidly respond to the questions below? Your com- │
│  ments will be given to me by the individual designated below; │
│  s/he will not reveal your name. Your comments will be used for │
│  advising purposes only. Thank you. │
│                                              │
│  *What are my strengths?*                    │
│                                              │
│                                              │
│                                              │
│                                              │
│  *What weak areas might I need to improve?*  │
│                                              │
│                                              │
│                                              │
│  *In your opinion, what do I need in a job or career to make me* │
│  *satisfied?*                                │
│                                              │
│                                              │
│                                              │
│                                              │
│  Please return to: _____ │
│                                              │
└──────────────────────────────────────────────┘
```

- *Strong-Campbell Interest Inventory*
- *Career Assessment Inventory*
- *The Self-Directed Search*
- *Temperament and Values Inventory*
- *Sixteen Personality Factor Questionnaire*
- *Edwards Personal Preference Schedule*
- *Myers-Briggs Type Indicators*
- *Self-Description Inventory*

C. *From yourself:* Numerous alternatives are available for you to practice redundancy:

1. Identify your work values or *"satisfiers"* by checking the items which pertain to you in this *"Identifying Your Work Values"* exercise:

─── IDENTIFYING YOUR WORK VALUES ───

I prefer employment which enables me to:

___ contribute to society	___ be creative
___ have contact with people	___ supervise others
___ work alone	___ work with details
___ work with a team	___ gain recognition
___ compete with others	___ acquire security
___ make decisions	___ make a lot of money
___ work under pressure	___ help others
___ use power and authority	___ solve problems
___ acquire new knowledge	___ take risks
___ be a recognized expert	___ work at my own pace

Select four work values from the above list which are the most important to you and list them in the space below. List any other work values (desired satisfactions) which were not listed above but which are important to you:

1. _____

2. _____

3. _____

4. _____

_____

2. Develop a comprehensive list of your past and present *job frustrations and dissatisfactions*. This should help you identify negative factors which should be avoided in future jobs. Use *"My Job Frustrations and Dissatisfactions"* form to develop this list:

── MY JOB FRUSTRATIONS ── AND DISSATISFACTIONS

List as many past and present things that frustrate or make you dissatisfied and unhappy in job situations:

Rank

1. _____ ____

2. _____ ____

3. _____ ____

4. _____ ____

5. _____ ____

6. _____ _____

7. _____ _____

8. _____ _____

9. _____ _____

10. _____ _____

3. Brainstorm a list of *"Ten or More Things I Love to Do"*. Identify which ones could be incorporated into what kinds of work environments:

——TEN OR MORE THINGS I LOVE TO DO——

To the right of each item you list, indicate what work environment best relates to the particular item:

	Item	*Related Environment*
1.	_____	_____
2.	_____	_____
3.	_____	_____
4.	_____	_____
5.	_____	_____
6.	_____	_____
7.	_____	_____
8.	_____	_____
9.	_____	_____

10. _____   _____

    _____   _____

    _____   _____

4. List *"Ten Things I Enjoy the Most About Work"* and rank each item accordingly:

——TEN THINGS I ENJOY—— THE MOST ABOUT WORK

Rank

1. _____ ____

2. _____ ____

3. _____ ____

4. _____ ____

5. _____ ____

6. _____ ____

7. _____ ____

8. _____ ____

9. _____ ____

10. _____ ____

5. Your *"Interpersonal Environments"* of work are extremely important. Identify the types of people you like and dislike associating with:

INTERPERSONAL ENVIRONMENTS

Characteristics of people
I like working with:

_____

_____

_____

_____

_____

_____

_____

_____

_____

Characteristics of people
I dislike working with:

_____

_____

_____

_____

_____

_____

_____

_____

_____

STEP 3: *Project your values and preferences into the future by completing simulation and creative thinking exercises:*

A. *Ten Million Dollar Exercise:* First, assume that you are given a $10,000,000 gift; now you don't have to work. Since the gift is restricted to your use only, you cannot give any part of it away. What will you do with your time! At first? Later on? Second, assume that you are given another $10,000,000, but this time you are required to give it all away. What kinds of causes, organizations, charities, etc. would you support?

WHAT WILL I DO WITH —— TWO $10,000,000 GIFTS?

First gift is restricted to my use only:

_____

_____

_____

_____

Second gift must be given away:

_____

_____

_____

_____

SOURCE: John C. Crystal, *"Life/Work Planning Workshop."* (Boston, Massachusetts, September, 1975).

B. *Obituary Exercise:* Make a list of the most important things you would like to do or accomplish before before you die. Two alternatives are available for doing this. First, make the list in response to this lead-in statement: *"Before I die, I want to . . ."*

BEFORE I DIE, I WANT TO . . .

1. _____

_____

2. _____

_____

3. _____

_____

4. _____

_____

5. _____

_____

6. _____

_____

7. _____

_____

8. _____

_____

9. _____

_____

10. _____

_____

Second, write a newspaper article which is actually your obituary for ten years from now.

Stress your accomplishments over the coming ten year period.

— MY OBITUARY —

Obituary for Mr./Ms. _____ to appear in the _____ Newspaper in 19 __.

_____

_____

_____

_____

_____

_____

_____

_____

_____

_____

_____

_____

_____

C. *My Ideal Work Week:* Starting with Monday, place each day of the week on the headings of seven sheets of paper. Develop a daily calendar with 30-minute intervals, beginning at 7am and ending at mid-night. Your calendar should consist of a 119-hour week. Next, beginning at 7am on Monday (sheet one), identify the *ideal activities* you would enjoy doing, prefer doing, or need to do for each 30-minute segment during the day. Assume you are capable of doing anything; you have no constraints except those you impose on yourself. Furthermore, assume that your work schedule consists of 40 hours per week. How will you fill your time? Be specific.

——— MY IDEAL WORK WEEK ———

Monday
am   pm

7:00 _____   4:00 _____

7:30 _____   4:30 _____

8:00 _____   5:00 _____

8:30 _____   5:30 _____

9:00 _____   6:00 _____

9:30 _____   6:30 _____

10:00 _____   7:00 _____

10:30 _____   7:30 _____

11:00 _____   8:00 _____

11:30 _____   8:30 _____

12:00	_____	9:00	_____
p.m.	_____	9:30	_____
12:30	_____	10:00	_____
1:00	_____	10:30	_____
1:30	_____	11:00	_____
2:00	_____	11:30	_____
2:30	_____	12:00	_____
3:00	_____	Continue for Tuesday, Wednesday, Thursday, and Friday	
3:30	_____		

D. *My Ideal Job Description:* Develop your ideal future job. Be sure you include:

- Specific interests you want to build into your job.
- Work responsibilities.
- Working conditions.
- Earnings and benefits.
- Interpersonal environment.
- Working circumstances, opportunities, and goals.

Use *"My Ideal Job Specifications"* on page 118 to outline your ideal job. After completing this exercise, synthesize the job and write a detailed paragraph which describes the kind of job you would most enjoy (use *"Description of My Ideal Job"* form on page 119):

MY IDEAL JOB SPECIFICATIONS

job interests	work responsibilities	working conditions	earnings/ benefits	interpersonal environment	circumstances/ opportunities/ goals

```
┌──────── DESCRIPTION OF MY IDEAL JOB ────────┐
│                                             │
│   ───────────────────────────────────────   │
│                                             │
│   ───────────────────────────────────────   │
│                                             │
│   ───────────────────────────────────────   │
│                                             │
│   ───────────────────────────────────────   │
│                                             │
│   ───────────────────────────────────────   │
│                                             │
│   ───────────────────────────────────────   │
│                                             │
│   ───────────────────────────────────────   │
│                                             │
└─────────────────────────────────────────────┘
```

STEP 4: *Test your objective against reality. Evaluate and refine it by conducting market research, a force field analysis, library research, and informational interviews.*

A. *Market Research:* Four steps are involved in conducting this research:

1. *Products or services:* Based upon all other other assessment activities, make a list of what you *do* or *make*:

```
┌──────── PRODUCTS/SERVICES ────────┐
│            I DO OR MAKE            │
│                                   │
│   1.  ─────────────────────────   │
│                                   │
│   2.  ─────────────────────────   │
│                                   │
│   3.  ─────────────────────────   │
│                                   │
│   4.  ─────────────────────────   │
│                                   │
└───────────────────────────────────┘
```

5. _____

6. _____

7. _____

8. _____

9. _____

10. _____

2. *Market:* Identify who needs, wants, or buys what you do or make. Be specific. Include individuals, groups, and organizations. Then, identify *what* specific *needs* your products or services fill. Next, assess the *results* you achieve with your products or services.

THE MARKET FOR MY PRODUCTS/SERVICES

Individuals, groups, organizations needing me:

1. _____

2. _____

3. _____

4. _____

5. _____

Needs I fulfill:

1. _____

2. _____

3. _____

4. _____

5. _____

Results/Outcomes/Impacts of
my products/services:

1. _____

2. _____

3. _____

4. _____

5. _____

3. *New Markets:* Brainstorm a list of *who else* needs your products or services. Think about ways of expanding your market. Next, list any new needs your current or new market has which you might be able to fill:

———— DEVELOPING NEW NEEDS ————

Who else needs my products/services?

1. _____

2. _____

3. _____

4. _____

5. _____

New ways to expand my market:

1. _____

2. _____

3. _____

4. _____

5. _____

New needs I should fulfill:

1. _____

2. _____

3. _____

4. _____

5. _____

4. *New products and/or services:* List any new products or services you can offer and any new needs you can satisfy:

—— NEW PRODUCTS/ ——
SERVICES I CAN OFFER

1. _____

2. _____

3. _____

4. _____

5. _____

——— NEW NEEDS I CAN MEET———

1. _____

2. _____

3. _____

4. _____

5. _____

B. *Force Field Analysis:* Once you have developed a tentative or firm objective, force field analysis can help you understand the various internal and external forces affecting the achievement of your objective. Force field analysis follows a specific sequence of activities:

- Clearly state your objective or course of action.

- List the positive and negative forces affecting your objective. Specify the internal and external forces working *for* and *against* you in terms of who, what, where, when, and how much. Estimate the impact of each force upon your objective.

- Analyze the forces. Assess the importance of each force upon your objective and its probable affect upon you. Some forces may be irrelevant to your goal. You may need additional information to make a thorough analysis.

- Maximize positive forces and minimize negative ones. Identify actions you can take to strengthen positive forces and to neutralize, overcome, or reverse negative forces. Focus on the key forces which are real, important, and probable.

- Assess the feasibility of attaining your objective and, if necessary, modifying it in light of new information.

C. *Conduct Library Research:* This research should strengthen and clarify your objective. Consult various reference materials on alternative jobs and careers:

Career and Job Alternatives:	• *Dictionary of Occupational Titles* • *Encyclopedia of Careers & Vocational Guidance,* William E. Hopke (ed.) • *Guide for Occupational Exploration* • *Occupational Outlook Handbook* • *Occupational Outlook Quarterly*
Industrial Directories:	• *Bernard Klein's Guide to American Directories* • *Dun and Bradstreet's Middle Market Directory* • *Dun and Bradstreet's Million Dollar Directory* • *Encyclopedia of Business Information Sources* • *Geography Index*

	• *Poor's Register of Corporations, Directors, and Executives*
	• *Standard Directory of Advertisers*
	• *The Standard Periodical Directory*
	• *Standard and Poor's Industrial Index*
	• *Standard Rate and Data Business Publications Directory*
	• *Thomas' Register of American Manufacturers*
Associations:	• *Directory of Professional and Trade Associations*
	• *Encyclopedia of Associations*
Government Sources:	• *The Book of the States*
	• *Congressional Directory*
	• *Congressional Staff Directory*
	• *Congressional Yellow Book*
	• *Federal Directory*
	• *Federal Yellow Book*
	• *Municipal Yearbook*
	• *Taylor's Encyclopedia of Government Officials*
	• *United National Yearbook*
	• *United States Government Manual*
	• *Washington Information Directory*
Newspapers:	• *The Wall Street Journal*
	• Major city newspapers
	• Trade newspapers
	• Any city newspaper --

especially the Sunday
edition.

Business   • *Barron's, Business Week,*
Business World, Forbes,
Fortune, Harvard Business
Review, Money, Time,
Newsweek, U.S. News
and World Report

Other library   • Trade journals (refer to
the *Directory of Special*
Libraries and Information
Centers and *Subject*
Collections: A Guide to
Specialized Libraries of
Businesses, Governments,
and Associations).
• Publications of Chambers
of Commerce; State
Manufacturing Associa-
tions; and federal, state,
and local government
agencies
• Telephone books -- The
Yellow Pages
• Trade books on *"How to*
get a job"

4. *Conduct Informational Interviews:* This
may to be the most useful way to clarify
and refine your objective. The procedure
for this is outlined in Chapter Ten.

After completing these steps, you will have identified what it is you
can do (abilities and skills), enlarged your thinking to include what it is
you would *like* to do (fantasies), and probed the realities of implementing
your objective. Thus, setting a realistic work objective is a function of the
diverse considerations represented on page 127.

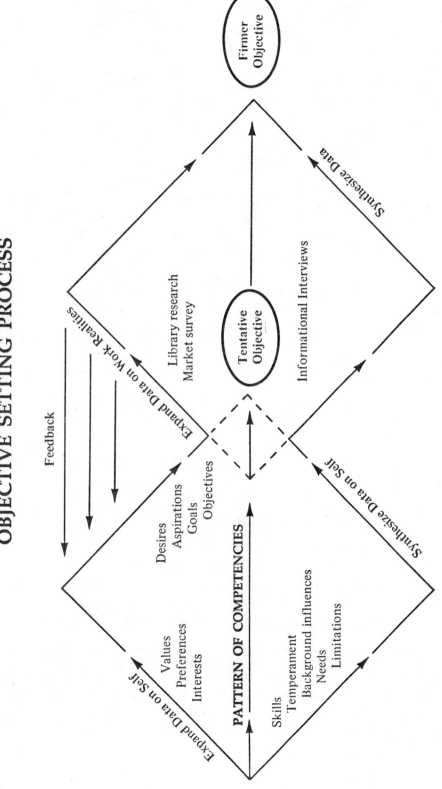

OBJECTIVE SETTING PROCESS

Firmer Objective

Tentative Objective

Synthesize Data

Library research
Market survey

Informational Interviews

Expand Data on Work Realities

Feedback

Objectives
Goals
Aspirations
Desires

Synthesize Data on Self

PATTERN OF COMPETENCIES

Values
Preferences
Interests

Skills
Temperament
Background influences
Needs
Limitations

Expand Data on Self

Your work objective is a function of both subjective and objective information as well as idealism and realism. We believe the strongest emphasis should be placed on your competencies and should include a broad data-base. Your work objective is realistic in that it is tempered by your past experiences, accomplishments, skills, and current research. An objective formulated in this manner permits you to think beyond your past experiences.

Stating a Functional Objective

Your job objective should be oriented toward skills and results or outcomes. You can begin by stating a functional job objective at two different levels: a general objective and a specific one for your resume. For the general objective, begin with the statement:

── STATING YOUR GENERAL OBJECTIVE ──

I would like a job where I can use my ability to _____

which will result in _____ .

SOURCE: Richard Germann and Peter Arnold, **Bernard Haldane Associates**
            Job & Career Building (New York: Harper and Row, 1980), 54-55.

The objective in this statement is both a **skill** and an **outcome**. For example, you might state:

── SKILLS-BASED AND ── RESULTS-ORIENTED OBJECTIVE

I would like a job where my experience in program development, supported by innovative decision-making and systems engineering abilities, will result in an expanded clientele and a more profitable organization.

At a second level you may wish to re-write this objective in order to target it at various consulting firms. For example, on your resume it becomes:

TARGETED OBJECTIVE ON RESUME

An increasingly responsible research position in consulting, where proven decision-making and system engineering abilities will be used for improving organizational productivity.

The following are examples of weak and strong objective statements. Various styles are also presented:

WEAK OBJECTIVES

Management position which will utilize business administration degree and will provide opportunities for rapid advancement.

A position in social services which will allow me to work with people in a helping capacity.

A position in Personnel Administration with a progressive firm.

Sales Representative with opportunity for advancement.

STRONG OBJECTIVES

*To use computer science training in **software development** for designing and implementing operating systems.*

A public relations position which will maximize opportunities to develop and implement programs, to organize people and events, and to communicate positive ideas and images. Effective in public speaking and in managing a publicity/promotional campaign.

A position as a General Sales Representative with a pharmaceutical house which will use chemistry background and ability to work on a self-directed basis in managing a marketing territory.

A position in data analysis where skills in mathematics, computer programming, and deductive reasoning will contribute to new systems development.

Retail Management position which will use sales/customer service experience and creative abilities for product display and merchandising. Long term goal: Progression to merchandise manager wiht corporate-wide responsibilities for product line. Willing to travel and relocate.

Responsible position in investment research and analysis. Interests and skills include securities analysis, financial planning, and portfolio management. Long range goal: to become a Chartered Financial Analyst. Willing to travel and relocate.

Your objective should be work-centered, not self-centered.

It is important to relate your objective to your audience. While you definitely want a good job, your audience wants to know what you can do for them. Remember, your objective should be work-centered, not-self-centered.

DESCRIBING EXPERIENCE

Begin compiling information your past experiences by using the forms on pages 132-134. Include paid employment; full-time, part-time, and summer employment; internships; and significant volunteer work. Refer to the data-base you generated previously for identifying your abilities and skills and stating your objectives. Make multiple copies of these forms.

When transforming this data to *"experience"* statements on your resume, avoid listing formal duties and responsibilities. Describe your experience in functional terms as outlined in our section on transferable skills and objectives. Always stress your accomplishments. Use action verbs in outlining your experience and qualifications, such as *"managed"*, *"created"*, *"supervised"*, *"coordinated"*, *"planned"*, *"analyzed"*, and *"initiated"*. Be sure everything you state here is related to your objective.

Your experience statements will vary depending on the type of resume format you use. For example, in a chronological resume, your experience may be stated as follows:

EXPERIENCE STATEMENT FOR CHRONOLOGICAL RESUME

EMPLOYMENT: *Engineering Draftsman.* Naval Electronics Systems Engineering Command, San Diego, California. Worked with engineers and technicians in developing electrical diagrams and schematics (1987 to present).

Draftsman with Dominion Sheetmetal Corporation, Washington, DC. Became familiar with manufacture of NVAC systems. Designed prototype of equipment for employer. Twenty hours per week (1986).

In a functional resume you may choose to use the terms "EXPERIENCE" or "AREAS OF EFFECTIVENESS" instead of "EMPLOYMENT" or "WORK HISTORY". In this case you will describe your transferable skills in functional terms without mentioning formal titles and dates. This section may appear on your resume as follows (page 138):

EMPLOYMENT EXPERIENCE WORKSHEET

1. Name of employer: _____

2. Address: _____

   _____

3. Inclusive dates of employment: From _____ to _____.
   month/year   month/year

4. Type of organization: _____

5. Size of organization/approximate number of employees: ___

6. Approximate annual sales volume or annual budget: _____

7. Position held: _____

8. Earnings per month/year: _____

9. Responsibilities/duties: _____

   _____

   _____

   _____

10. Achievements or significant contributions: _____

    _____

    _____

    _____

    _____

11. Demonstrated skills and abilities: _____

    _____

    _____

12. Reason(s) for leaving: _____

    _____

— MILITARY EXPERIENCE WORKSHEET —

1. Service: _____

2. Rank: _____

3. Inclusive dates: From _____ to _____.
   month/year   month/year

4. Responsibilities/duties: _____

   _____

   _____

   _____

   _____

5. Significant contributions/achievements: _____

   _____

   _____

   _____

   _____

   _____

6. Demonstrated skills and abilities: _____

   _____

   _____

   _____

   _____

   _____

7. Reserve status: _____

COMMUNITY/CIVIC/
VOLUNTEER EXPERIENCE

1. Name and address of organization/group: _____

_____

_____

_____

2. Inclusive dates: From _____ to _____.
                          month/year   month/year

3. Offices held/nature of involvement: _____

_____

_____

_____

_____

4. Significant contributions/achievements/projects: _____

_____

_____

_____

_____

5. Demonstrated skills and abilities: _____

_____

_____

_____

```
┌─────────── EXPERIENCE STATEMENT ───────────┐
│                FOR FUNCTIONAL RESUME        │
│                                             │
│              AREAS OF EFFECTIVENESS         │
│                                             │
│ Planning/      Planned, organized, and delegated responsibility │
│ organizing     for several successful fund raising projects. Es- │
│                tablished objectives and planned yearly budget │
│                which involved balancing club objectives and │
│                community needs. Coordinated and planned │
│                summer camps for handicapped children which │
│                gained favorable recognition. │
│                                             │
│ Managing/      Coordinated and scheduled individuals for ac- │
│ directing      tivities such as the Bloodmobile and the │
│                Community Health Center. Solicited and evalu- │
│                ated applicants for club scholarship award. │
│                                             │
│ Interpersonal/ Developed liaison relationship between city offi- │
│ communication  cials and people in the community. Established │
│                support of the local business community for │
│                club projects. │
└─────────────────────────────────────────────┘
```

The combination resume will include both functional cataegories and work history. However, "EXPERIENCE" or "AREAS OF EFFECTIVENESS" should appear first and "EMPLOYMENT HISTORY" last.

PRESENTING EDUCATIONAL BACKGROUND

A statement in reference to your educational background can appear anywhere after your objective, depending on how much you wish to emphasize it in relationship to your objective and experience. If you appear over or under educated for a job, you may wish to de-emphasize your training by placing the education category near the end. Again, where you place this item depends on your purpose.

The same is true for deciding what to include in the education statement. If you are a recent graduate with little work-related experience, you may want to highlight those educational achievements which indicate

COMBINATION RESUME FORMAT

NAME
address
telephone number

_____

OBJECTIVE   _____

_____

_____

AREAS OF EFFECTIVENESS

**Planning/
organizing**   _____

_____

_____

**Managing/
directing**   _____

_____

_____

**Interpersonal/
communication**   _____

_____

_____

**EMPLOYMENT
HISTORY:**   Mathematics Teacher, Peoria Junior High School,
                         Peoria, Illinois, 1987 to present.
                    Administrative Assistant, U.S. Government, Fort
                         Monroe, Virginia, 1984-1986.

EDUCATION: _____

_____

ability to achieve results, such as *"edited conference papers"*, *"financed 80% of personal expenses"*, *"held leadership positions in various organizations"*, and *"maintained a 3.5 GPA on a 4.0 index"*. Whatever you choose to include, begin by compiling as much information on your education and training as possible and then condense it in relationship to your objective. Complete copies of the *"Education Data"* form on page 138 for this purpose.

The education statement can appear in different forms. But remember, you are trying to get everything on one page. Your objective and experience categories will be more important to readers than your education statement. So plan accordingly by not making this category excessively large. Examples of education statements are as follows:

──── EDUCATION STATEMENTS ────

EDUCATION: *B.S. in Business Administration* -- Accounting, 1990, University of North Carolina, Chapel Hill.

           Highlights: G.P.A.: 3.6 (4.0 index)
                       Earned 75% of education and personal expenses. Member, Accounting Club.

EDUCATION: M.A., Journalism, Columbia University, 1990.
                  B.A., English Literature, Barnard College, 1988.

If you have training other than formal degrees and diplomas, and it is pertinent to your objective, you may wish to include it in a section immediately following "EDUCATION" and label it "ADDITIONAL TRAINING":

──── EDUCATION AND ADDITIONAL ──── TRAINING STATEMENT

EDUCATION: **B.S. in Business Administration** -- Accounting, 1985. University of North Carolina, Chapel Hill.

ADDITIONAL TRAINING: Zero-Base Budgeting, Army Budgeting I, Commercial Accounts, Introduction to Data Processing, Personnel Management.

EDUCATIONAL DATA

1. **Institution:** _____

2. **Address:** _____

   _____

3. **Inclusive dates:** From _____ to _____.
                    month/year   month/year

4. **Degree or years completed:** _____

5. **Major:** _____ **Minor(s):** _____

6. **Education highlights:** _____

   _____

   _____

7. **Student activities:** _____

   _____

   _____

8. **Demonstrated abilities and skills:** _____

   _____

   _____

   _____

9. **Significant contributions/achievements:** _____

   _____

   _____

10. **Special training courses:** _____

    _____

11. **G.P.A.:** _____ (on _____ index)
                        point

MAKING PERSONAL STATEMENTS

You may want to disregard this section altogether since it remains one of the most tradition-bound and non-functional sections on resumes. If you include it, keep it brief and to the point. Avoid extraneous information, such as your height, weight, hair color, state of health, and other personal characteristics, unless they are essential to your job objective. In some cases this information merely raises negative questions. If you are single, divorced, or separated, so what? Your sex and marital life are not your employer's business -- unless you or they make it so. However, if you are single, and you are applying for a job requiring considerable travel, identifying your marital status can be a plus in your favor. On the other hand, if a job requires stability, and you are married and have children, you may include your marital status -- but don't include the names of your children, even though you are proud of them! As for age, if it will help, put it down. Leave your age off altogether if it serves no useful purposes, particularly if you are middle-aged or over.

You may wish to include some other personal information for strengthening your objective. For example, your personal data could include the following:

```
┌─────────────── PERSONAL STATEMENT ───────────────┐
│                                                   │
│  PERSONAL:    35 . . . in excellent health . . . married . . . │
│               children . . . enjoy challenges . . . interested │
│               in productivity.                    │
│                                                   │
└───────────────────────────────────────────────────┘
```

Alternatively, you could write a personal statement about yourself so that the reader might remember you in particular. However, avoid trite statements. For example,

```
┌─────────────── SPECIAL INTERESTS STATEMENT ───────────────┐
│                                                           │
│  SPECIAL      Love the challenge of solving problems, taking │
│  INTERESTS:   initiative, and achieving results . . . be it in │
│               developing new marketing strategies, program-  │
│               ming a computer, climbing a mountain, white    │
│               water rafting, or modifying a motorcycle.      │
│                                                           │
└───────────────────────────────────────────────────────────┘
```

Such statements can give hobbies and special talents and interests new meaning in relationship to the resume objective.

INCLUDING REFERENCES

Never list your references on your resume. Always control these yourself. Be sure to inform your references of your job search activities. Give them a copy of your resume so they understand your objective and qualifications.

When deciding whether to include a reference section on your resume, you essentially have two choices: leave this section off altogether, since it is an empty category without names, or use the following statement:

REFERENCE STATEMENT

REFERENCES: Available upon request

We see no useful purpose served by stating this. It merely takes up valuable space that can be allocated to a more thorough presentation of your qualifications. If you drop this category completely, most readers will assume you will make your references available upon request. Employers will ask you for references when the time is right -- which usually is during the interview. Sometimes they don't ask for references or don't contact the individuals on your list. However, it is good practice to list the names of your professional references on a separate sheet of paper; carry the list with you to interviews. The list should be typed and should contain the full name, title, business, address, and telephone number of each person.

DECIDING ON MISCELLANEOUS INFORMATION

You may wish to include other information on your resume: special skills, professional memberships and affiliations, and hobbies. If you have special licenses or special training and skills (can program a computer, invented the laser gun) relevant to your job objective, include this information on your resume. If you are actively involved in a professional organization -- hold an office or organized a program -- and it is relevant to your qualifications, include it on your resume with appropriate statements to emphasize your role. Membership alone is not particularly impressive. Most people understand the nature of professional memberships and affiliations: you do little other than write a check for your annual dues.

Hobbies, like your height and weight, seldom enhance your objective and some distract by raising unnecessary questions about your sanity or *"normality"*! Nonetheless, you may engage in some hobbies or activities that will strengthen your professional and personal marketability, such as writing books, articles, and speeches -- or composing music. Such hobbies stress your organizational, communication, and creative abilities. Other hobbies may leave a lasting positive impression on the reader and thus he or she will remember you in particular. But swimming, collecting stamps, and playing cards may communicate the wrong things -- you're a jock, withdrawn, or a gambler.

Never, never, never put your salary expectations on your resume. Salary is the last thing you discuss in a job interview, and it is negotiable.

You should complete the *"Additional Information"* forms on pages 142-143 so you will at least have this information available for reference. After compiling information on these miscellaneous categories, include in the resume only those items which enhance your objective and qualifications. Again, your purpose is to produce as much information on your background and qualifications as possible and then condense it into a one or two-page resume draft. It is much easier to condense than to expand such information.

ADDITIONAL INFORMATION

1. **Professional memberships and status:**

    a. _____

    b. _____

    c. _____

    d. _____

    e. _____

2. **Licenses/certifications:**

    a. _____

    b. _____

    c. _____

3. **Expected salary range:** $ _____ to $ _____ (but do not include this on your resume)

4. **Acceptable amount of on-the-job travel:** _____
    days per month

5. **Areas of acceptable relocation:**

    a. _____   c. _____

    b. _____   d. _____

6. **Date of availability:** _____

7. **Contacting present employer:**

    a. Is he or she aware of your prospective job change? _____

    b. May he or she be contacted at this time? _____

8. **References:** (name, address, telephone number – not to appear on resume)

    a. _____   c. _____

    b. _____   d. _____

9. **Foreign languages and degree of competency:**

    a. _____

    b. _____

10. **Interests and activities:** hobbies, avocations, pursuits

    a. _____

    b. _____

    c. _____

    d. _____

    e. _____

Circle letter of ones which support your objective.

11. **Foreign travel:**

	Country	Purpose	Dates
a.			
b.			
c.			
d.			

12. **Special awards/recognition:**

a.			
b.			
c.			
d.			

13. **Special abilities/skills/talents/accomplishments:**

    a. _____

    b. _____

    c. _____

Chapter Eight

PUT IT TOGETHER
WITH IMPACT

Armed with the information you compiled in Chapter Seven, you should be well prepared to write first and second drafts of your resume. The drafting process involves producing each section of the resume in reference to specific evaluation criteria as well as re-working it until the finished product looks first-class.

DOING FIRST AND SECOND DRAFTS

Your first resume draft will directly evolve from the information you put together on the data forms in Chapter Seven. Take several sheets of paper and at the top of each write the title of one resume category: OBJECTIVE, EDUCATION, EXPERIENCE, PERSONAL. Refer to your master data forms as you write each category as you want them to appear on your resume. As you do this, keep in mind two questions:

- Does this information strengthen my objective as well as demonstrate my strengths?

- Is the language crisp, succinct, and expressive?

Your choice of language is important throughout this process. Be sure to use action verbs to enhance the readability of each section and to strengthen the presentation of your abilities and skills. Work and re-work each sentence until the statements are concise and meaningful in reference to your objective. Remember, less is often more when writing your resume. You want to edit, edit, edit, edit! If, for example, your objective statement is written in six or seven lines, keep editing until it is no more than three lines. You can say just as much -- if not more -- and say it better in three lines than in six. Resume writing gives you a license to rid yourself of useless language in order to communicate clearly and with impact.

---

*Less is often more when writing
your resume. When in doubt,
throw it out.*

Always keep in mind your objective *and* audience when deciding what to include in each section. A good rule to follow is: When in doubt, throw it out. Otherwise, you will have difficulty putting all the essential information on one or two pages.

After completing the individual sheets, arrange each category into a chronological, functional, or combination format, according to our advice in Chapter Seven and following our examples in Appendices A and B. At this stage your resume probably will be more than one page -- but not more than two pages. If necessary, eliminate the less important categories, such as "PERSONAL" and "REFERENCES."

You should subject your initial draft to both internal and external evaluations. An *internal evaluation* examines the proper form and content of your resume. An *external evaluation* involves circulating your draft resume to at least three individuals who will critique it in terms of its strengths and weaknesses. Choose individuals who have hiring expertise. We examine both types of evaluations in the next section.

Your second draft should incorporate the results of the internal and external evaluations. At this point you should subject your resume to major surgery to further condense it into a one to two-page format. Keep editing until you eliminate extra pages. Again, follow our rule for condensing resume content – *"when in doubt, throw it out"*.

After completing the second draft, conduct another external evaluation by circulating the new resume to the same individuals who critiqued your first draft. In addition, contact three other individuals with hiring experience; ask them also to critique this draft. If all goes well, your second draft will become the final resume. If not, revise again by incorporating this new audience feedback. Circulate it again and again until your final product receives high marks from your evaluators.

Writing resumes is a skill or competency you develop through experience.

It is critical to field test your drafts in this manner. While you may need to further revise your resume in response to new advice and information on the job market, these preliminary trial runs should get you started in the right direction. Writing resumes is a skill or competency you develop through experience. The more extensive your experience, the better your final product.

CONDUCTING INTERNAL AND EXTERNAL EVALUATIONS

It is important to conduct both internal and external evaluations of your resume. The *internal evaluation* identifies and rates the strengths and weaknesses of your resume. Be sure to follow each weak rating with a note to yourself specifying how you will correct the particular problem. This activity enables you to evaluate *and* follow-through in revising the resume. Refer to the evaluation form on pages 147-148 to conduct your internal evaluation.

You conduct an *external evaluation* by circulating your resume to three or more individuals. Choose people whose opinions are objective, frank, and thoughtful. Do not select friends and relatives who usually flatter you with positive comments. Professional acquaintances or people

INTERNAL RESUME EVALUATION

Characteristics	Very Strong	Strong	So-so	Weak	Very Weak	Action Needed
1. Overall appearance...						
a. makes an immediate favorable impression	1	2	3	4	5	_____
b. is inviting to read	1	2	3	4	5	_____
c. is easy to read	1	2	3	4	5	_____
d. looks professional	1	2	3	4	5	_____
2. Contact information...						
a. is clearly presented at the top	1	2	3	4	5	_____
b. includes address information	1	2	3	4	5	_____
c. includes telephone number(s)	1	2	3	4	5	_____
3. Objective...						
a. is stated clearly and conveys purpose	1	2	3	4	5	_____
b. emphasizes strongest qualifications which are likely to match employers' needs	1	2	3	4	5	_____
c. is reasonably short (2-3 lines)	1	2	3	4	5	_____
4. Organization...						
a. has strongest qualifications presented immediately after the objective	1	2	3	4	5	_____
b. emphasizes strongest points	1	2	3	4	5	_____
c. presents layout consistently	1	2	3	4	5	_____

5. **Content. . .**

a. supports and substantiates objective   1   2   3   4   5 _____
b. stresses skills, accomplishments, and
    results rather than duties and
    responsibilities   1   2   3   4   5 _____
c. is free from extraneous material   1   2   3   4   5 _____
d. conveys productive use of time   1   2   3   4   5 _____

6. **Language. . .**

a. expressed in succinct manner   1   2   3   4   5 _____
b. uses action verbs to begin phrases   1   2   3   4   5 _____
c. has short action-oriented phrases
    instead of full sentences   1   2   3   4   5 _____
d. is free from grammatical, spelling,
    and punctuation errors   1   2   3   4   5 _____
e. is in active rather than passive voice   1   2   3   4   5 _____

7. **Length. . .**

a. is brief — not more than two pages   1   2   3   4   5 _____

COMMENTS:

you don't know personally but whom you admire may be good evaluators. An ideal evaluator has experience in hiring people in your area of job interest. In addition to sharing their experience with you, they may refer you to other individuals who would be interested in your qualifications. If you choose such individuals to critique your resume, ask them for their frank reaction -- not what they would politely say to a candidate presenting such a resume. You want the people to role play with you -- a potential interview candidate. Ask your evaluators:

- Why wouldn't they invite you to an interview given this draft of your resume?

- If they, as employers, were writing your resume, what changes would they make -- additions, deletions, modifications?

You will normally receive good cooperation and advice by approaching people in this manner. In addition, you will probably get valuable unsolicited advice on other job search matters, such as job leads, job market information, and employment strategies.

In contrast to the closed and deductive nature of the internal evaluation, the external evaluation should be open-ended and inductive. Avoid preconceived evaluation categories; let the evaluator react to you and your resume as if you were in a job interview situation. Taken together, the internal and external evaluations should complement each other by providing you with maximum information for revising your draft resume.

PRODUCING A FIRST-CLASS RESUME

When you are ready to produce the final resume, you must consider quality *and* cost. Both will influence the effectiveness of your resume. Do not cut quality because of costs, since differences in resume quality amount to only a few dollars. On the other hand, don't go to the extreme with a slick Madison Avenue advertising brochure. You may threaten some employers with your overkill approach; others may think you are lazy because they assume you hired a professional resume writing service to do your work; still others may suspect you are hiding weaknesses.

Production techniques will vary depending on your targeted audience. If you are competing with 500 applicants for a position, your resume must stand out from the crowd. This may mean producing a non-conventional resume. Hopefully you will not be competing with so many applicants. Indeed, if you seek non-publicized job opportunities, only *your* resume will stand between you and a prospective employer.

Let's assume you will apply for publicized and highly competitive positions as well as look for unpublicized job opportunities which have little competition. In both cases, your resume should respond to the type of position you are seeking. It should look professional, be eye appealing, and stand out from other resumes. You do this by following various guidelines and techniques for producing an outstanding resume.

Word Processor and Typewriter Produced

You can home-produce your resume on a word processor or on an electronic typewriter which uses a letter quality printer or interchangeable typing elements and a carbon ribbon. Dot matrix printers and cheap quality machines produce amateurish looking resumes. By using a letter quality printer or a typewriter with interchangeable elements and a carbon ribbon, you can achieve a professional looking resume which also communicates your personal style. In addition, you maintain the flexibility to make any internal alterations without incurring the expenses of a typesetter. Most word processors or typists with access to such equipment can do your resume for $15-20.

Typesetting

The major alternative to home production is typesetting. Most printers can typeset and print a master copy of your resume. Typesetting may cost you $40 per page or more. While you will achieve a very professional looking resume, typesetting has its negatives:

- Costly

- Your lose control and flexibility to change elements in the resume.

- It may appear *too* professional or or too slick and thereby give employers a negative impression — you were too lazy to write your own resume, even though you did it yourself!

Use your own good judgment about typesetting the resume. Again, know your audience. Some audiences prefer the extreme professional look whereas others like the home-produced professional look. Your external evaluation should answer this question for you.

If you typeset your resume, be sure to proofread the master copy. Typesetters do make mistakes. You don't want to learn about these mistakes after sending copies to employers.

Layout and Use of Space

Your resume should have a crisp and clear look which is visually pleasing to the reader. You achieve this by using white space frequently yet sparingly. Avoid the crammed and crowded look; the more blank space you leave around each section, the better. Section headings should be arranged to the left or above each section. Separate each section with at least one and a half spaces -- preferably two. Use a series of periods (ellipsis) to break sentences and ideas on the same line (. . .). You may want to type each section separately and then clip and paste into different layouts until you achieve the visual effects you desire. The use of single and double lines to accent sections and a full or partial border drawn along the edge of the resume can give it an unusual effect which also looks very professional.

Highlights and Emphasis

You can emphasize various elements in your resume by arranging space, using different lettering styles (or typing elements) and symbols (* o ● + -), capitalizing, underlining and using bold print for words, phrases, and sentences. However, careful not to over-emphasize in this manner; many readers do not like having their reading flow broken so frequently. If you do a good job at editing your resume you will not need to highlight points so frequently by using such techniques.

Paper

Use high quality stock which has a first-class look and feel. Bond paper will cost 2¢ to 6¢ per sheet. It can be purchased through major stationery stores and printers. Use at least a 20-pound weight -- the heavier the better.

Color

We prefer a conservative off-white, ivory, light tan, or light grey paper to other colors. During the past decade, the best resumes were considered to be one-page, typeset resumes printed on high quality off-white or beige paper. Since so many resumes are now produced in these colors, they no longer stand out as unique or different. Indeed, the standard black and white resume often stands out among the many off-white resumes!

Although we used to prefer the off-white and beige colors, we now prefer the light grey with dark blue, navy, or black print. Whatever you choose, avoid extremes, such as bright red, pink, orange, or green. Conservative, light muted colored papers with dark inks are your best choices. However, if you are an artist or are in some other less conventional career, choose a color that best expresses your professional goals, personality, and style. Furthermore, if you are competing with hundreds of other applicants and wish to stand out from the crowd, you may wish to take your chances with a less conservative paper color. Knowing your audience is your best guide to selection of colors and designs. But when in doubt, go with conservative colors.

When dealing with employers who do not know you, assume they will be conservative and cautious. They look for symbols of your personality, style, and performance *prior to* inviting you to an interview. Regardless of the content of your resume -- experience, education, objective -- your choice of resume colors and style give employers nonverbal cues for screening you in or out of consideration for an interview.

Reproduction

Reproduce your resume by using an offset process or a high quality copying machine that gives you as good as, if not better than, original quality reproduction. The offset process is relatively inexpensive -- from 2 to 5 per copy with runs of 100 or more -- and the quality is usually very good. Make sure your original has dark, clear type, and no errors. Do not type your master on erasable bond or onion skin paper since it is very difficult to get quality reproductions from this type of paper. Use white liquid correction fluid to cover any undesired marks or smudges on your original. Remind your printer to produce only *perfect copies.*

Producing your resume in this manner will be relatively inexpensive and will look very professional. Whatever you do, plese *do not* get cheap at this stage by (1) making copies of your resume on a chintzy copy machine, or (2) substitute 2¢ a sheet mimeograph paper for 3¢ a sheet high quality, off-white bond paper. At best you will probably save $5 on 100 copies. This is not the place to cut corners since your resume is your calling card for getting interviews. Pay the extra pennies, nickels, and dimes required to produce a first-class professional resume. You will be more than rewarded in the end for incurring such limited additional costs.

EVALUATING THE FINAL PRODUCT

Similar to evaluating your first and second drafts, you should evaluate the final resume both internally and externally. The external evaluation takes place as you conduct your job search with actual employers. If you have difficulty getting feedback on your resume, ask employers for comments and advice. In so doing, they will read your resume in greater depth and you will gain valuable advice to incorporate into your resume.

Conduct your internal evaluation by completing the form on page 154. Be sure to note in the right-hand column any action you need to take in order to improve the quality of your resume.

How can you produce a professional looking resume when the competition is doing the same? Simply don't compete with the same product. Make your resume look professional and *different*. Follow the guidelines in this chapter and vary the layout as well as the quality and color of paper.

Your final resume should approximate one or two of the resume examples found in Appendices A and B. While you should refer to these examples, under no circumstances should you copy their contents. Your resume must reflect *your* goals and strengths. Moreover, it should indicate the fact that *you* produced it. By all means avoid producing another *"canned"* resume.

PRODUCTION EVALUATION

Characteristics	Very Strong	Strong	So-so	Weak	Very Weak	Action Needed
1. Production. . .						
a. is unusually attractive	1	2	3	4	5	_____
b. looks professional	1	2	3	4	5	_____
c. allows for flexibility to alter elements in resume	1	2	3	4	5	_____
2. Layout and space utilization. . .						
a. is crisp and clean	1	2	3	4	5	_____
b. incorporates white space	1	2	3	4	5	_____
c. separates sections for easy reading	1	2	3	4	5	_____
d. is unique yet acceptable and professional	1	2	3	4	5	_____
3. Highlighting and emphasis. . .						
a. gives overall pleasing visual effect	1	2	3	4	5	_____
b. uses symbols, underlining, different letter styles and sizes, and capitalizes headings	1	2	3	4	5	_____
c. is well balanced — does not use highlighting and emphasis too frequently	1	2	3	4	5	_____
4. Paper. . .						
a. is high quality bond	1	2	3	4	5	_____
b. weighs 20-pounds or more	1	2	3	4	5	_____
c. is off-white, ivory, light tan, light grey, or other conservative and conventional color	1	2	3	4	5	_____
d. will stand out from the crowd	1	2	3	4	5	_____
5. Reproduction. . .						
a. is clear, clean, and professional	1	2	3	4	5	_____
b. provides you with enough copies	1	2	3	4	5	_____

Chapter Nine

COMMUNICATE WITH EFFECTIVE LETTERS

You should write several types of letters during your job search: resume, cover, approach, and thank-you. While this chapter mainly focuses on how to develop effective resume and cover letters, it also briefly examines other types of letters which are equally important to your job search.

Letters are similar in purpose to resumes: your advertisement for interviews and job offers. High impact letters combine the principles of effective advertising copy with good business correspondence. Your letters, like good ads and business communication, should command the attention and positive response of your audience.

Writing letters with impact is similar to writing good advertising copy. While some English teachers and journalists may help you develop these letters, it is best to consult advertising books or freelance copywriters who are specialists on *how to write with impact*.

HAVING IMPACT

Your letter writing should follow various principles of good advertising and effective business correspondence. This involves a simple three-step formula for writing well: *think, write,* and *edit.* Effective writers devote time to each of these steps.

A well-known formula for writing successful ads stresses:

- Use an eye-catching headline to capture the reader's attention.

- Capture and sustain the reader's interest by persuasively describing and explaining the benefits of your product or service.

- Create additional credibility and desire by presenting evidence, testimonials, or further explanations of the value of your product or service.

- Stimulate action for the order or purchase.

You can adapt these advertising principles to your letter writing by first addressing these questions:

- Who is my audience?

- What is my objective?

- What are the objectives and needs of my audience?

- How can I best express my objective in relationship to my audience's objectives and needs?

- What specific benefits can I offer to my audience and how can I best express them?

- What opening sentence and paragraph will grab the attention of my audience in a positive manner and invite them to read further?

- How can I maintain and heighten the interest and desire of the reader throughout the letter?

- What evidence can I present of my value to my audience?

- If a resume is enclosed with the letter, how can I best make the letter advertise the resume?

- What closing sentence or paragraph will best assure the reader of my capabilities and persuade him or her to contact me for further information?

- Is the letter my *best* professional effort?

- Have I spent sufficient time drafting, revising, and proofreading the letter before sending it to the reader?

At the same time, your letter is more than an advertisement. It is your business communication. Therefore, you must present yourself in a professional business-like manner by incorporating the principles of effective business correspondence in your resume. Eight rules generally define these principles:

┌─ GOOD BUSINESS CORRESPONDENCE RULES ─┐

1. Plan and organize what you will say by outlining the content of your letter.

2. Know your purpose and plan the elements of the letter accordingly.

3. Communicate your message in a logical and sequential manner.

4. State your purpose immediately in the first sentence and paragraph; main ideas always go first.

5. End your letter by stating what your reader can expect next from you.

6. Use short paragraphs and sentences; avoid complex sentences.

7. Punctuate properly and use correct grammar and spelling.

8. Use simple and straightforward language; avoid jargon. Communicate your message as directly and briefly as possible.

The first five rules help you *organize* your letter. The final three rules stress how you should *communicate* your message. Underlying these rules is an advertising principle you should follow at all times: *know your audience's needs and keep your purpose in mind.*

You can achieve impact by using different writing styles or by communicating the unexpected. Some candidates use unorthodox styles to get attention. For example, career counselors tell the story of the young man who sent a shoe in a box to a company executive with this accompanying one-sentence letter:

"Now that I've got my shoe in the door, how about an interview?"

John Molloy (*Live for Success*) recalls receiving a letter from a woman applying for a secretarial job with his company:

"You know I don't have a great deal of experience, and I know I've worked for several companies in the last few years and that may not look good. But I guarantee you one thing. If I do come to work for you I'll work like hell!"

This letter definitely had impact. Molloy was initially turned off by her language, but it struck him as honest and powerful. He interviewed her and took a chance by hiring her. But all did not go well:

"She did work like hell. She spelled like the devil, showed up when she felt like it, and gave everyone around her a lot of heat. As a result I had to let her go in a few weeks. But she did know how to sell herself in a cover level."

We do not recommend such hard sell, kinky, or unorthodox letters, unless the situation is appropriate for them. If you are applying for a sales position, for instance, your letter may be somewhat aggressive and unorthodox because of the nature of sales positions. After all, employers expect a high turnover rate among sales people. Employers are willing to take chances, because most sales people are low cost employees who are paid on the basis of their performance. However, the hard sell, aggressive, and unorthodox letter may get you in trouble for a non-sales position. For example, send your shoe with a letter to the head of an accounting department and see what happens. Or, apply for a management position by broadcasting how you work like hell and are the greatest thing since sliced bread! Job search letters should have impact, but they should not be over-bearing.

CREATING RESUME LETTERS

As noted in Chapter Six, resume letters can substitute for chronological, functional, and combination resumes. Use this letter to communicate your specific skills and qualifications directly to someone in an organization. The letter should follow the same rules for writing a good resume.

Resume letters have one major advantage over cover letters and resumes: you can customize them to target specific positions. These letters provide you with flexibility. This is especially true if you run multiple copies of a general resume but need to alter its contents for particular jobs.

A resume letter should be addressed to a name *and* title. Type the letter on good quality bond paper and keep it within one-page. The internal organization of this letter should approximate the following format and rules:

— GOOD RESUME LETTER ORGANIZATION—

Paragraph 1:   Clearly state your purpose for writing.

Paragraph 2:   Stress your objective, interests, and qualifications in relationship to the individuals' interests and possible needs. This paragraph substitutes for the "EXPERIENCE" or "AREAS OF EFFECTIVENESS" sections of your resume and should follow similar writing principles.

Paragraph 3:   Request to meet with the individual to discuss your mutual interests. Indicate that you will call to arrange a meeting.

We include several examples of these letters in Appendix C.

Your resume still plays an important role in the job search process even when you use a resume letter. While most job seekers send resumes with cover letters for getting interviews, the resume letter is designed to get the interview without an accompanying resume. In this case, the resume is presented at the *end* of the interview.

The resume letter may have greater impact on potential employers because it is targeted. However, since many employers expect to see resumes prior to inviting candidates to interviews, a resume letter may not be well received by employers who want more information. Again, use your own judgment as to when you should best use this letter in lieu of your resume.

WRITING COVER LETTERS

Cover letters should do precisely what they are intended to do -- provide cover for an enclosure. The enclose is your resume. If you want your reader to examine your resume, your cover letter must have impact. This letter advertises your resume; it should neither regurgitate nor substitute for it.

This (cover) letter advertises your resume; it should neither regurgitate nor substitute for it.

Some career counselors recommend against writing and sending cover letters with resumes. They believe these letters distract from the resume; a cover letter, in effect, downgrades the resume. As an alternative, they recommend handwriting a personal note at the top of your resume which states you will telephone the employer at a particular time to make an appointment for an interview. If you do this many times -- such as *"shotgun"* 200 resumes -- you will get results -- perhaps three to five appointments and interviews. Indeed, in many cases this approach can work. The keys to making it work are (1) playing the probability game of sending many resumes in anticipation of only a few positive responses, and (2) following the resume and handwritten note with a telephone call. In this case, the *telephone call* substitutes for the cover letter. This approach has one major advantage: it saves you the trouble of writing and typing many cover letters. However, a disadvantage is also apparent: high costs of long-distance telephone calls.

Nonetheless, at times you must write cover letters because they are expected in certain situations. If you are *"shotgunning"* resumes, it makes sense to eliminate the cover letter because it saves additional typing on your part and requires less reading for employers. But *"shotgunning"* is only one approach to uncovering job leads. As we note in Chapter Ten, it is not the most effective way to find a job. More frequently you will respond to job listings or uncover unpublicized job opportunities by sending a resume accompanied by a cover letter. In these situations, a cover letter is necessary. Since you have written a high impact resume, your cover letter should complement the resume with additional impact.

The cover letter should be viewed as an advertisement to learn more about the *"product"*, which is outlined in the resume. In other words, your cover letter advertises your advertisement. It should provide the initial sizzle. It captures the reader's attention, stresses the employer's needs and your value, and invites him or her to read the resume in-depth. The resume, in turn, repeats the process of grabbing attention and stressing value. Moreover, the resume sustains and heightens the reader's interest. It provides additional credibility by detailing your value in relationship to your goals and the employer's needs.

Similar to other types of letters, your cover letters should follow certain general rules:

COVER LETTER RULES

1. *Type on good quality bond paper.*

2. *Address to a specific name and title.* If you are uncertain whom to address, look in library reference materials or call the company and ask the receptionist for an appropriate name and title. For openers, tell the receptionist:

   "I am sending some important papers to the head of the ____ _____ Department. However, I'm not sure I have the correct name and address. Could you please tell me to whom I should address these documents?"

3. *Writing style should be direct, powerful, and error free.* Edit to eliminate extraneous words and to check grammar, spelling, and punctuation. In addition to stating your purpose, the letter tells the reader how well you communicate.

4. *No more than one page.* Do not overwhelm the resume with a lengthy cover letter or excessive repetition of the resume content.

5. *Keep the letter short and to the point.* Three paragraphs will suffice:

> Paragraph 1:   State your interest and purpose. Try to link your interests to the employer's needs.
>
> Paragraph 2:   Highlight your enclosed resume by stressing what you will do for the employer.
>
> Paragraph 3:   Request an interview and indicate you will call for an appointment.

6. *Use appropriate language.* Repeat terms the employer uses. Avoid jargon and the passive voice. Use action verbs as well as the active voice. Don't try to be cute or too aggressive.

7. *Always be positive* by stressing your past accomplishments and skills as well as your future value.

Examine the cover letter on page 163. The letter is written in response to a specific job vacancy. It is purposeful without being overly aggressive or boastful. The writer's purpose is already known by the employer. The first paragraph should re-state the position listed as well as the source of information. It links the writer's interests to the employer's needs. The writer also indicates some knowledge of the organization. Overall, the first paragraph is succinct, purposeful, and thoughtful. The writer invites the reader to learn more about him.

In the second paragraph the writer generates additional interest by referring to his enclosed resume and including additional information for emphasizing his qualifications vis-a-vis the employer's needs. The writer also attempts to re-write the employer's ad around his qualifications. In so doing, this writer should stand out from other candidates because he *raises* the expectations of the employer beyond the position description. The writer, in effect, suggests to the employer that he or she will be getting more for their money than anticipated. At the same time, the paragraph does not appear hyped, boastful, or aggressive. It is low-keyed yet assertive.

In the third paragraph of this example, the writer makes an open-ended offer to the employer which is difficult to refuse. Linking his interest to the reader's, the writer softens the interview request without

HIGH IMPACT COVER LETTER

931 Davis Street
Boston, MA 01931
January 18, 19___

John F. Baird, Manager
Hopkins International Corporation
7532 Grand Avenue
Boston, MA 01937

Dear Mr. Baird:

Your listing in the January 17 issue of the *Daily News* for a managerial trainee interests me for several reasons. I possess the necessary experience and skills you outline in the ad. Your company has a fine reputation for quality products and a track record of innovation and growth. I seek a challenging position which will fully use my talents.

My experience and skills are summarized in the enclosed resume. You may be interested in several additional qualifications I would bring to this position:

- the ability to relate well to others
- a record of accomplishments and a desire to achieve better results
- a willingness to take on new responsibilities
- enthusiasm and initiative

I would appreciate more information concerning this position as well as an opportunity to meet with you to discuss our mutual interests. I will call you Thursday morning concerning any questions we both may have and to arrange an interview if we deem it is appropriate at that time.

I appreciate your consideration and look forward to meeting you.

Sincerely yours,

Steven L. Reeves

putting the employer on the spot of having to say *"yes"* or *"no"*. Overall, the writer presents the employer with an opportunity to examine his *value*. Accompanied with an outstanding resume, this letter should make a positive impression on the employer. A phone call within 48-hours of receiving the letter will further enhance the writer's candidacy.

For additional examples of cover letters, refer to Appendix C.

PRODUCING APPROACH LETTERS

An approach letter is a letter designed to gain access to individuals who may or may not provide you with contacts, leads, and information on job opportunities. These letters are also used for building networks which may lead to informational interviews (Chapter Ten).

An approach letter is a letter designed to gain access to individuals who may or may not provide you with contacts, leads, and information on job opportunities. These letters are also used for building networks which may lead to informational interviews (Chapter Ten).

Approach letters are associated with two major job search strategies. The first strategy involves conducting an indiscriminate mass mailing of hundreds of resumes and cover letters to specific individuals in your area of interest. If you follow-up your direct mailing with telephone calls, you will get results.

While some individuals report impressive results with this version of the shotgun method, we do not endorse it with enthusiasm. Employers are being flooded with hundreds and thousands of such resumes and phone calls. The entry of copy machines and word processors into the job search process has led to a tremendous increase in such mass mailings over the past few years. As employers become increasingly inundated with slick resumes and cover letters -- many from professional job search firms -- this strategy will become less effective.

The second strategy involves selectively writing letters to prospective employers or to individuals who might provide you with useful job search information and referrals. Normally you should not include your resume with this letter. Instead, take your resume to the informational interview and discuss it near the end of the interview. This is done for two purposes: (1) gathering advice on how to improve your resume, and (2) getting the interviewer to read your resume as well as refer it to others who might be interested in your qualifications.

With this second strategy you tailor the contents of the letter to your audience. However, certain common elements should appear in the letters.

APPROACH LETTER RULES

1. *Start with a personal statement which connects you to the reader.* If you lack a personal referral, you might open with: *"I am writing to you because of your position as..."* or *"Because of your experience in..."*, or *"We have a common interest in..."*, or *"Since we are both alumni of _____ I thought..."* If you have a referral, you might start with: *"Mr., Mrs., Dr., Professor_____ suggested that I contact you..."*

2. *Orient the reader to your purpose.* Explain that you do not expect the reader to know of any current job openings, but you would like his or her help, advice, suggestions, or guidance. Stress your purpose(s): to get his or her advice on your career plans, obtain occupational information, or discuss future work possibilities. Explain your current situation.

3. *Close your letter by requesting a brief meeting* at a mutually convenient time. Indicate that you will call in a few days to arrange a meeting.

4. *Be clear.* Have a specific purpose in mind before writing this letter.

5. *Always address the letter to a name,* never to a position or title.

6. *Make your letter brief,* unless there are special reasons for going into detail.

7. *Make your letters warm and personal.* Avoid officious, stereotyped, or jargonistic language.

8. *Carefully proofread* for grammatical, spelling, or typing errors.

9. *Neatly type your letter.* Leave wide margins. Use a new typewriter ribbon or carbon ribbon. If you use a word processor, print the letter on a letter quality printer.

10. *Type on good quality bond stationery.* Never use erasable, copy machine, or onion-skin paper.

11. *Keep copies of all correspondence* in an efficient filing system for follow-up purposes (see Chapter Ten)

For examples of approach letters, see Appendix C. While numerous additional examples are found in resume writing books, never copy or edit such letters for your use. Follow our general rules, target your specific audience, and convey your message in your own way.

Thoughtful people are remembered . . . You want to be remembered in a positive manner.

ADDING IMPACT WITH THANK-YOU LETTERS

When was the last time you received a thank-you letter or note from someone you helped or who came to your party or dinner? Chances are you receive few such letters. Furthermore, you remember those you receive, and you tend to have a positive impression of the individuals who sent them. Why? Because they are *thoughtful* people.

Thoughtful people are remembered. When conducting a job search you should always strive to stand out from other candidates. A thank-you letter is one of the most effective letters you can write. You normally should write this letter within 48-hours following an interview. Thank-you letters also can be used in other types of situations, such as responding to advice over the telephone or a letter of rejection. Thank people for their advice, time, and consideration. Interestingly enough, some people report receiving job offers after being first rejected because they sent a nice thank-you letter.

We include different examples of thank-you letters in Appendix C. A *standard* thank-you letter should immediately follow a formal job interview. This letter highlights your interview discussion and reiterates your qualifications and continuing interest.

Thank-you letters in reference to *telephone conversations and informational interviews* should follow a similar format. Keep the letters short, be concise, reiterate major points of the conversation, and express your gratitude for assistance.

The thank-you letter in response to a *rejection* should follow a similar format. Express your gratitude for being considered for the position as well as your continuing interest in working with the employer. Few employers receive this type of letter. Hence, it may leave a lasting impression on the employer who will remember you for future openings.

Other types of thank-you letters also are appropriate to write at times. For example, if you *withdraw from consideration* for a position or turn down a job offer, send a polite and positive thank-you letter which leaves the door open for future consideration. Once you receive a *job offer*, send a thank-you letter to your new employer. This can be one of the most effective letters in getting you off to a good start and forming a positive and lasting relationship with your new employer. Since few employers receive such letters, you will stand out as a thoughtful and considerate new employee.

If you *terminate* employment for any reason, consider sending a thank-you letter to your former employer. Try to be as positive as possible, even though you may be parting under strained circumstances. A thank-you letter can clear the air, mend broken fences, generate positive references, and leave the door open for future reconsideration.

You should write these different types of thank-you letters because you want to be *remembered* in a positive manner. You communicate your thoughtful and considerate style. Coupled with your paper qualifications, as evidenced in your outstanding resume, you will achieve a degree of impact few candidates ever display in their job search. You will stand out in the crowd. Better yet, you may avoid the crowd altogether!

Chapter Ten

DISTRIBUTE, MARKET, AND MANAGE YOUR COMMUNICATION

Your resume and letters are only as effective as the quality of your distribution, marketing, and management systems. Some of the best resumes and letters are ineffective because individuals neglect to develop and manage these systems.

Now that you have your resume and letters in hand, what are you planning to do with them? Shotgun them to 500 personnel offices or key executives? Pass them around to friends and relatives? Hide them from people you know? Regardless of how you distribute them, how will you measure the effectiveness of your marketing campaign? What records do you need to keep, and how can you best organize your records in order to manage your marketing campaign?

These questions may seem minor compared to the importance of writing the resume and letters. However, if you neglect distribution and marketing activities, you may blame your failures on the quality of your resume and letters. More often than not, the problems lie in how you link your documents to your audience. Neglect marketing and distribution and you will effectively kill your job search campaign.

168

CHASING AFTER POT LUCK

You can distribute your resume and letters through different channels. The most apparent channel is the publicized job market of classified ads and vacancy announcements of personnel offices and employment agencies. While this is the least effective channel, it is still used by most people as their primary channel. You will encounter *high competition* there, and it will give you a *misleading picture* about employment opportunities. For example, you may get the impressions that *"there are few jobs available"*, *"getting a job is really tough these days"*, and *"there are so many other well qualified candidates -- I don't have enough experience"*. Don't invest more than one-third of your marketing time responding to publicized listings. Your time is better spent on higher payoff activities.

Neglect marketing and distribution
and you will effectively kill
your job search campaign.

Nonetheless, you should focus some of your job search efforts in this traditional employment channel. Jobs do exist there, and you could get lucky applying for one. Read the classified ads, but have realistic expectations. Job listings may be the least accurate gauge of the number and types of jobs available for someone with your qualifications. Most vacancy announcements normally fall into one of four categories:

1. Jobs that are difficult to fill by informal means because they (a) offer low wages, (b) require a high level of technical skills and experience, or (c) face a labor shortage in a particular occupation or geographical area.

2. Jobs that go unfilled because employers are relatively ignorant about how to hire; instead, they are forced into using the publicized channels.

3. Jobs which are already filled or *"wired"* by informal means but are listed in order to fulfill affirmative action and equal oppor-

tunity requirements.

4. Non-existent jobs — the blind ad where someone tests the waters or is collecting resumes for future reference.

You may encounter one or more of these situations if you respond to publicized job listings. Since many others will be applying simultaneously, your chances of getting an interview for a legitimate job are very slim. After sending resumes and letters in response to 100 ads, you may get five interviews -- if you are lucky!

The publicized job market remains a game of probability and chance. It is full of false hopes, dashed expectations, and disappearing job opportunities.

The best way to respond to want ads is to send a resume and letter addressed to a particular individual. If this is not possible because the ad lacks a name, address, or phone number, omit the saluation and write the body of the letter according to our suggestions in Chapter Nine. Wherever possible, get a phone number and call the individual about four to five days after sending your resume and cover letter. Restate your interest in the job and stress your value; request an interview at a mutually convenient time. Regardless of the outcome of this telephone conversation, send a thank-you letter immediately in which you (1) stress your gratitude for the individual's time, (2) highlight your qualifications, (3) reemphasize important points discussed in your conversation, and (4) reaffirm your interest in the position.

By injecting the use of the telephone and thank-you letter along with your resume, this approach to publicized job listings should increase your probability of getting an interview. However, it may only increase it from 5 to 10 percent. The publicized job market remains a game of probability and chance. By all means do not become too ego involved with this market. It is full of false hopes, dashed expectations, and disappearing job opportunities. Concentrate your major efforts on other distribution and marketing channels which should prove more effective and fruitful.

PENETRATING THE HIDDEN JOB MARKET

Anywhere from 60 to 80 percent of all jobs are found on a hidden job market. These jobs are not publicized in traditional channels and few job seekers know how to find them. There is *less competition* for these jobs and the *rewards tend to be greater* than those for publicized jobs.

Being unpublicized, this job market requires a creative strategy for effectiveness. You must use your resume and letters to open doors which may or may not produce useful information, job leads, interviews, and offers. The uncertainty and unpredictability of this job search channel may initially frustrate you because it is difficult to know when you are making progress. Instead, you invest your time in increasing the probabilities of uncovering job opportunities and interviews.

SHOTGUNNING

You can market yourself several ways in the hidden job market. First, you can *"shotgun"* organizations and individuals with resumes and letters. This is the least effective way of penetrating the hidden job market, but it will yield results -- if you play the numbers game. Send out 100 resumes and expect maybe one interview. Send out 200 resumes and expect maybe three interviews. If you persist long enough -- and can afford the mailing costs -- you will get more and more interviews which may lead to job offers. But don't send out 50 resumes and letters and expect results. You are playing the odds at their worst with this approach. The normal response will be a polite *"thank you"* letter indicating *"There are no openings at present for someone with your qualifications. We will keep your resume on file for future reference."* This is a polite way of telling you that they may be throwing away your materials along with the many other unsolicited resumes and letters they regularly receive.

However, you can improve your *"shotgun"* odds by immediately following your resume and letter with a *phone call* (see Chapter Nine). In your telephone conversation stress, as you should in your letter, that you are seeking information and advice on opportunities for someone with your qualifications. Don't put the individual on the spot by asking for a job. Ask for information and hope you will get referred to others. Above all, you want to be remembered in case the employer would have, or would know of, an opening for you in the future.

PROSPECTING AND NETWORKING

A second method of penetrating the hidden job market is through prospecting, networking, and informational interviews. This should prove to be your most effective job search strategy. Prospecting is a technique for developing personal contacts which will expand into interpersonal networks for the purpose of yielding important job search information. Your resume and letters play an important role throughout these processes.

---

*From 60 to 90 percent of jobs
are found informally -- mainly
through friends, relatives,
and direct application.*

Identifying and Using Your Network

The interpersonal nature of the job search is well documented. Since the 1930s studies of blue collar, white collar, managerial, technical, and professional workers have found that no more than 20 percent of placements occur through formal mechanisms. From 60 to 90 percent of jobs are found informally -- mainly through friends, relatives, and direct application. The U.S. Department of Labor reports that 63.4 percent of all workers use informal methods. Even with the highly structured government recruiting procedures, informal mechanisms play an important role in acquiring government employment.

Studies consistently show that formal and impersonal communications are the least effective means of getting a job: advertisements, public and private employment agencies, and job listings provided by organizations. The most widely used and effective methods are informal and personal: personal contacts and direct application. The personal contact is the major job-finding method, used by over 60 percent of all job seekers.

Studies also note that both employers and employees *prefer* the informal and personal methods. Both groups believe personal contacts result in more in-depth, accurate, and up-to-date *information* which both groups need. Employers feel these methods *reduce* their recruiting *costs* and hiring *risks*. Individuals who use personal contacts are more *satisfied* with their jobs; those who find jobs using formal methods tend to have a greater degree of job dissatisfaction. Those using informal methods tend to have *higher incomes*, and their jobs are in the highest income brackets.

Insurance, real estate, and other direct-sales businesses use several face-to-face sales techniques which can be effectively adapted to your job search. The major techniques are *networking, pyramiding, and client referral systems*. Your job search goals and situations will be analogous to those of business:

1. Your goal is to sell an important high quality product -- yourself -- by shopping around for a good buyer.

2. The buyer wants to be assured, based upon previous performance and current demonstration, that he or she is investing in a high quality and reliable product.

3. Face-to-face communication, rather than impersonal advertising, remains the best way to make buying/selling decisions.

4. When buyer and seller exchange information on each other, the quality of information improves and the new relationship will probably be mutually supportive, beneficial, and satisfying.

The techniques of building networks, pyramids, and referrals are relatively easy to learn and use. However, you must first understand the nature of networks, pyramids, and referral systems. A network consists of you and people you know, who are important to you, and whom you interact with most frequently. Many of these people influence your behavior. Others may also influence your behavior but you interact with them less frequently. As illustrated on page 174, your network may consist of family friends, assisters, professional colleagues, follow workers, and your supervisor. Your network of relationships involves *people* -- not data, things, or knowledge of a particular subject area.

You begin using your network in the job search by asking several key questions:

YOUR NETWORK OF RELATIONSHIPS

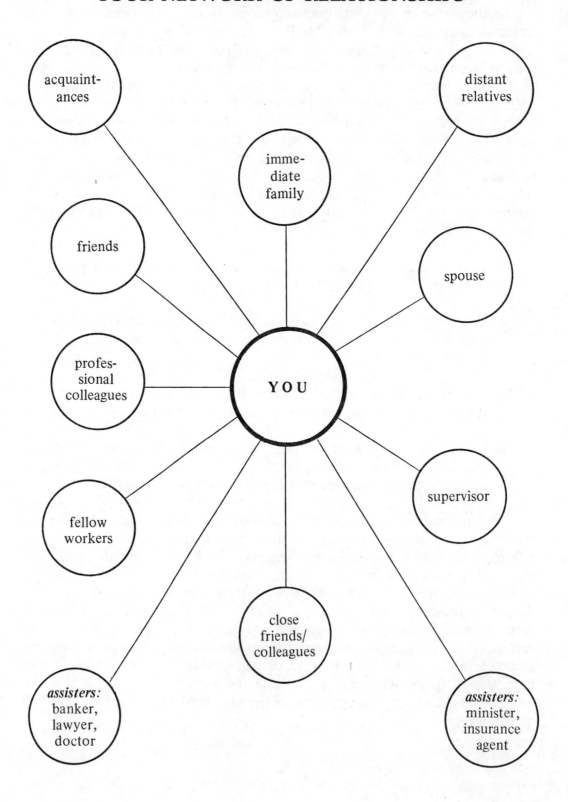

- Who can help you?

- Who has information related to your job objective?

- Who knows others who might be helpful?

Address these questions to individuals in your network. Since others in your network have their own networks, their *"contacts"* may be useful to you. If you contact someone for information and advice, this person probably will refer you to individuals in his or her network.

Since most people like to give advice (perhaps everyone has a secret desire to be Ann Landers!) and they know other people who can do the same, you will be linking your network to their networks. If you address the same question to your relative (Uncle Joe in Dallas) and a former, and highly successful classmate, you will create new *opportunity structures* for uncovering information for your job search. An example of linking your network to those of your colleague, relative, and former classmate is illustrated on page 176. If you extend your network to include individuals you do not interact with regularly, you will create an incredible number of network linkages.

Developing a Contact List

The best way to get started in prospecting and building networks is to develop a list of potential job search contacts. Begin by listing the names of all the people you know; include relatives, former employers, acquaintances, alumni, friends, bankers, doctors, lawyers, ministers, and professional colleagues. Perhaps only 15 of these people will be individuals you see and work with regularly. The others may be former friends, acquaintances, or your Aunt Betsy you haven't seen in ten years. If you have difficulty developing such a list, refer to the following checklist of categories to refresh your memory:

YOUR CONTACTS

[ ] Friends (take a look at your Christmas card list)
[ ] Neighbors (current and past)
[ ] Social acquaintances: golf, swim, tennis, social club members, PTA members
[ ] Classmates -- from any level of school
[ ] College alumni (get a list of those living locally)

```
[ ] Teachers -- your college professors, your children's teachers
[ ] Anybody you wroe a check to in the past year
    [ ] tradespeople, drugstore owner
    [ ] doctor, dentist, optician
    [ ] lawyer, accountant, real estate agent
    [ ] insurance agent, stock broker, travel agent
[ ] Manager of local branch of your bank
[ ] Co-workers and former co-workers
[ ] Relatives
[ ] Politicians (local leaders often are businessmen/women or
    professionals in town who know everybody.
[ ] Chamber of Commerce executives in town
[ ] Pastors, ministers (excellent resources)
[ ] Members of your church
[ ] Trade association executives
[ ] Professional organization executives
[ ] Members of your professional societies
[ ] People you meet at conventions
[ ] Speakers at meetings you've attended
[ ] Business club executives and members (Rotary, Kiwanis,
    Jaycees, etc.)
[ ] Representatives of direct-sales business (real estate,
    insurance, Amway, Shaklee, Avon)
[ ] Others
```

After developing your comprehensive list of contacts, classify the names into different categories of individuals:

- Those in influential positions or who have hiring authority

- Those with job leads

- Those most likely to refer you to others

- Those with long-distance contacts

Select at least 25 names from your list for initiating your first round of contacts. You are now ready to begin an active prospecting and networking campaign which should lead to informational interviews, formal job interviews, and job offers.

LINKING YOUR NETWORKS TO OTHERS

Organizing Your Networks

Prospecting involves contacting people in your network and building new networks for information and job leads. Many people in direct-sales quit at this point because they lack the prerequisites for success -- patience, perseverance, and a positive attitude. Prospecting techniques require you to:

- Develop enthusiastic one-on-one appointments and informational interview presentations.

- Be consistent and persistent in how you present your case.

- Give prospecting a high priority in your overall daily routine.

- Believe you will be successful given your persistence with these techniques; prospecting is a probability game involving both successes and failures.

Prospecting and networking, above all, requires *persistence*. For example, it takes about 20 minutes to initiate a contact by telephone -- longer by letter. If you contact at least one person in your immediate circle of contacts each day, your prospecting should yield 15 new contacts each week for a total investment of less than two hours. Each of these new contacts could possibly yield three additional contacts or 45 new referrals. However, some contacts will yield more than three and others may yield none. If you develop contacts in this manner, you will create a series of small pyramids, as illustrated on page 179. If you expand your prospecting from one to three new contacts each day, you could generate 135 new contacts and referrals in a single week. If you continue this same level of activity over a two-month period, it is possible to create over 1,000 new contacts and referrals! At this pace, your odds of uncovering job opportunities, being invited to formal job interviews, and receiving job offers will increase dramatically.

The linkages and pyramids on page 179 constitute your *job search network*. Always remember to nurture and manage this network so it performs well in generating information and job leads. As you follow-through on making new contacts, expect about half to result in referrals. However, a few of your contacts will continue to give you referrals beyond the initial ones. Consequently, you need to continually develop new contacts while maintaining communication with prior contacts. When

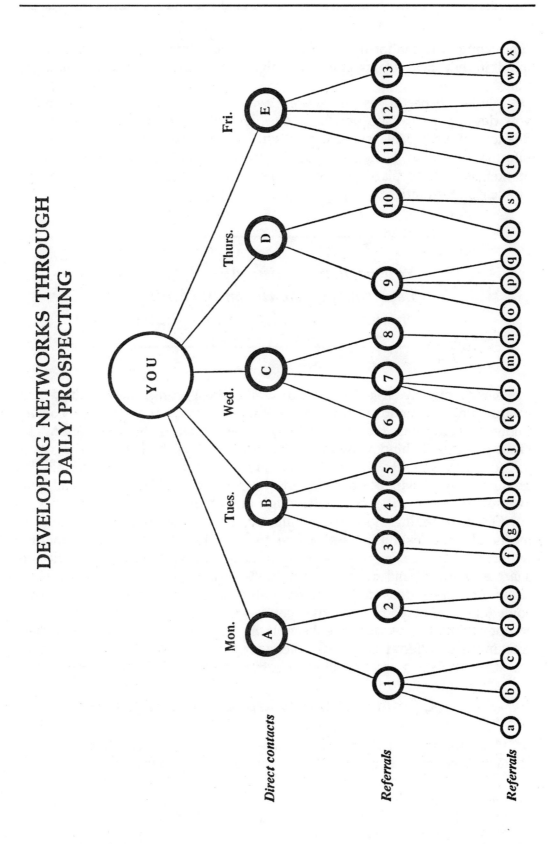

DEVELOPING NETWORKS THROUGH
DAILY PROSPECTING

conducting informational interviews ask your contacts to keep you in mind if they hear of anyone who might be interested in your qualifications.

While prospecting is an excellent way to create contacts, it also helps you develop a realistic objective, effective interview skills, and self-confidence. In using this system, you will seldom be turned down for an informational interview. You should uncover vacancies on the hidden job market as well as place yourself in a positive position to take advantage of such opportunities.

You need to continually develop new contacts while maintaining communication with prior contacts.

Never directly ask for a job while prospecting, networking, and conducting informational interviews. Asking for a job puts your contact under pressure; it is the quickest way to be politely shown the door. The basic principle behind networking is: the best way to get a job is never ask for a job directly; always ask for information, advice, and referrals. By doing this, you will be interviewed, your resume will be read, and you eventually will be offered a job through one or more of your contacts.

Our prospecting system is similar to the networking techniques used in the direct-sales businesses. These proven, low-keyed sales techniques require persistence, a personable approach to people, and the ability to share a *"product"* and offer an opportunity to prospective buyers. This low stress approach does not threaten individuals by asking them to buy something, or, in your case, give you a job. Some of the most successful businesses in the world have been built on this simple one-on-one networking and referral strategy. When adapted to the job search process, the same strategies have resulted in extremely successful job placements.

Conducting Informational Interviews

An informational interview is a low stress, face-to-face meeting with a contact or potential employer for the purposes of getting:

1. *Information* on present or future job opportunities in your interest and skill areas.

2. *Advice* on your job search campaign.

3. *Referrals* to other people who might be able to give you more information, advice, and referrals which, in turn, may lead to job interviews and offers.

At least 50 percent of your prospecting and networking should result in informational interviews.

The best way to get a job is never ask for a job directly; always ask for information, advice, and referrals.

Informational interviews have six major purposes:

PURPOSES OF ─── INFORMATIONAL INTERVIEWS

1. Gather current information on the job market relevant to your specific interests (labor market conditions, potentially interested employers, trends)

2. Acquire data on any known specific vacancies (nature of work, job titles, working environment, interpersonal and political climates)

3. Inform your contact of your interests and qualifications as well as get his or her reaction to your resume.

4. Get advice on how to proceed with your job search.

5. Obtain one or more referrals to others who can give you additional information and advice on potential vacancies and job market conditions.

6. Be remembered for future reference.

You should conduct informational interviews with two audiences: (1) individuals with useful occupational information, and (2) potential employers. Do not confine your contacts to a single level in an organization or assume that people at the top are the most knowledgeable. Individuals at other levels can be helpful too. Indeed, many middle-level managers know more about their organization and are more willing to talk with you than the influentials at the top. Furthermore, some organizations decentralize the hiring power to the operating units. Therefore, you must identify where to best target your efforts. There is no substitute for *knowing your organization.*

Why should influential people want to talk with you? They have any number of reasons to see you for an informational interview:

- Window-shopping for new talent

- Professional courtesy

- Superstition and fatalism

- Acquire information from you

- Relaxation

- Curiosity

- Recruiting for a friend

- Sounding-board -- test out his or her ideas on you

- Ego-needs to live up to your expectatons

- Desire to *"play God"*, and help those who help themselves

- Internal politics -- spread word on the grapevine that he or she is looking for new talent

- Need to save time and money

- Your persistence overcomes his or her resistance

- Unconscious fear -- *"there but for the grace of God go I"*

- Pay back the world -- he or she was once helped by others

- Reciprocity -- he or she may need you some day

- Genuine desire to help others

- Discover genius or hidden talent

- Enjoys opportunity to criticize

- Coincidence of timing -- he or she is actively looking

At the same time, be prepared to encounter individuals who may have another 20 reasons for not seeing you. In that case, you must reassess your approach, try again with these individuals, or move on to others.

The procedure for conducting an informational interview can vary depending on your audience. Some people are successful in conducting *"cold-turkey"* interviews with important *strangers* in key positions. Others follow a four-step process with great success:

┌─ INFORMATIONAL INTERVIEWING PROCESS ─┐

1. *Send an approach letter:* follow the advice outlined in Chapter Nine on writing this letter. Do not enclose your resume.

2. *Make a telephone appointment:* this follows a few days after sending your letter. Try to set a specific time and date for a meeting. Avoid conducting a telephone interview.

3. *Conduct the interview:* seek information, advice, and referrals. Leave a copy of your resume and ask to be remembered for future openings.

> **4.** *Send a thank-you letter:* be sure it is warm and sincere and follows the advice in Chapter Nine.

The structure of a one-on-one informational interview should remain fairly consistent. Develop a script that is low-keyed, yet assertive enough to clearly communicate your objective and enthusiasm. Prior to the actual interview, role play with a friend.

Remember that most people do not want to be put on the spot to be responsible for your employment fate. Therefore, try to promote a low stress situation and develop a futuristic orientation. Most people like to give advice and be helpful. They are flattered when you ask for advice because you are saying that you value their opinions and knowledge. Such compliments will most likely result in willing cooperation and useful information. Many contacts will want to see you achieve your goals.

While your primary purpose is to gather information about future job possibilities, you should not hide the fact that you are looking for a job -- if indeed you are. For example, you might say to your interviews: *"While I don't expect you to have a job vacancy now, I would like to talk to you about future opportunities."* Bluntly asking for a job may make the person feel uncomfortable and prematurely end your relationship.

Your informational interviews should focus on *seeking information on opportunities and advice on your job objective.* You need such information advice in order to make sound decisions about your future. Also, ask your contact to critique your resume and suggest how to proceed with your job search. Such a line of discussion should capture the empathy of your interviewer. After all, everyone has been involved in career planning and job hunting, and they will continue to do so in the future. You will find that most contacts will refer you to other individuals for further information and advice.

Questions and Dialogue

Informational interviews are conversations which yield specific types of information. While this interview appears somewhat unstructured, you should maintain a basic structure to keep a conversation flowing. Your discussion might approximate the following:

── INFORMATIONAL INTERVIEW DIALOGUE ──

INTRODUCTION: *"Mr. Roberts, hello. It's a pleasure to meet you, and I really appreciate your taking some time to see me."*

PURPOSE AND EXPECTATIONS: *"As I said in my letter to you, I am exploring different job and career opportunities. Your type of work interests me very much. I want to learn more about (technical writing, accounting, sales, personnel administration, etc.). Let me reiterate, I don't expect you to have or even know of a job vacancy."*

JOB REQUIREMENTS, RELATIONSHIPS, ENVIRONMENTS: *"If it's okay with you, I'd like to ask you some questions about this type of work:*

- *What's involved in (occupation) in terms of regular tasks and activities?*

- *What skills and abilities are required to do a good job?*

- *What kinds of relationships with others are expected or necessary in performing the job?*

- *What is the work environment like in terms of pressure, deadlines, routines, new activities?*

NOTE: discussion of work requirements should take 15-20 minutes

TRANSITION: *"This has been very helpful to me. You've given me information that I've not read nor even considered before."*

OCCUPATIONAL OUTLOOK AND APPLICATION ADVICE: *"I'd like to shift the focus a bit and ask your opinion about the employment outlook in (occupation):*

- *Are job prospects good, stable, or very competitive?*

- *What local organizations employ people in (occupation)?"*

- *What's the best way to apply for jobs in*

(_occupation_)?"

NOTE: discussion of employment outlook, job hunting, and application procedures should take approximately 10 minutes

RESUME
EVALUATION:

"If you don't mind, would you look over my resume? Perhaps you could comment on its clarity or make suggestions for improving it?"

OCCUPATIONAL
OPPORTUNITIES
FOR YOU:

"How would someone with my background get started in (_____)? What kinds of positions could I qualify for?"

GET REFERRED
AND
REMEMBERED:

"You've been most generous with your time, and the information you've given me is most useful. It clarifies and reinforces a number of points for me. I have two final requests:

- *The jobs you thought might be appropriate for someone with my skills sound interesting and I'd like to find out more about those possibilities. Do you know individuals in those kinds of jobs who would be willing -- like yourself -- to provide me with additional information?*

   NOTE: about half will provide you with multiple referrals

- *Finally, I would appreciate it if you could keep my resume for reference in case you hear of a vacancy appropriate for someone with my background and interests."*

EXPRESS
GRATITUDE:

"Thanks again for taking the time to see me. You've been very helpful and I appreciate it.

Being Thoughtful and Repeating

Upon completion of the informational interview, be sure to express your gratitude for the person's time and assistance. Make sure the person has your resume. Keep this interview to 30-45 minutes. However, don't be surprised if it runs longer than anticipated; many interviewers enjoy discussing their work and giving advice.

Within a day, write a thank-you letter (see Appendix C) in which you again express your gratitude for his or her assistance and emphasize once again that you would appreciate being kept in mind if he or she hears of any opportunities for someone with your qualifications. Some career consultants advise you to hand write this note; others tell you to type it since typing looks much more professional than handwriting. We think this the proverbial *"six one way, half a dozen another"* situation long as it is neat and readable. Do what best fits your style and your understanding of your audience. But be sure you send a thank-you letter.

Continue repeating the prospecting, networking, and informational interviewing. While your immediate goal is to get a job, your long-term goal is to build a career. Do not forget your contacts once you achieve your immediate objective. You owe them a debt of gratitude for helping you. After you get a job, inform them of your success and thank them once again for their assistance. In many cases, you may develop new and lasting relationships as a result of your job search.

---

*You, too, will be successful
in getting job interviews and
offers if you continue
prospecting, networking, and
conducting informational interviews.*

Expected Results

Our networking and informational interviewing approach is based upon years of successful experience with thousands of clients. Most major professional career counseling firms teach this method to their clients, and they report excellent results. You, too, will be successful in getting job interviews and offers if you continue prospecting, networking, and conducting informational interviews. The odds are in your favor as long as you constantly repeat these activities. In general, your odds are about 50 percent that employers will meet with you based upon your approach letter. At the end of informational interviews, expect another 50 percent to refer you to three or four others. Consequently, if you feel you need more contacts, informational interviews, and referrals, just increase the level of your prospecting and networking activities.

It is difficult to give precise estimates as to when you can expect your first formal job interview and offer based upon this approach. Some people get lucky and follow-through on their first referral with an informational interview that yields a job offer. Others repeat these activities for four to six months before receiving a job offer. A realistic prospecting plan is to initiate one new contact each day. Within the first month, you will have developed your initial contacts and completed your first round of informational interviews. During the second month, the number of informational interviews should increase considerably. Within two and a half to three months, firm job offers should be forthcoming. Again, job offers can occur at any time, from your first informational interview to your 100th interview six months later. But if you are consistent in making five new contacts each week and following-through on your referrals, you should begin receiving job offers within two and a half to three months.

KEEPING RECORDS

As you begin applying for many positions and networking for informational interviews, you will need to rely on something more than your memory. A good record-keeping system can help you manage your job search effectively.

One of the simplist and most effective systems consists of recording data on 4 x 6 cards. If you respond to classified ads, clip the ad and paste it to the card. Label the card in the upper left hand corner with a useful reference category and subcategory. For example, in applying for a management trainee position with a food company, your category might appear as follows: MANAGEMENT TRAINEE -- food. In the upper right hand corner, place the name of the company. At the bottom of the card identify the name, title, address, and phone number of your contact person. This side of the card should appear as the example on page 189.

On the reverse side of the same 5 x 6 card, record all information pertinent to making contacts for this position. Organize this information by dates and the nature of the contact. Add any information which documents your continuing contacts. For example, this side of your card might look like the second card on page 189.

MANAGEMENT TRAINEE --   GENERAL FOODS
    food

(ad)

Mr. James Lathrop
General Manager
4291 Grand Master Blvd.
Chicago, Illinois 60221
(815)223-8012

7/9/90 --	sent resume (#14) with cover letter to Mr. Lathrop.
7/13/90 --	telephoned Mr. Lathrop to set up interview for 7/22. Spoke with secretary, Jean Staples.
7/18/90 --	received letter from Mr. Lathrop confirming appointment time and requesting information.
7/22/90 --	interviewed with Mr. Lathrop. See GENERAL FOODS file. Sent thank-you letter to Mr.Lathrop.
7/25/90 --	offered position at $35,000
7/27/90 --	telephoned Mr. Lathrop to decline offer.
7/28/90 --	sent letter thanking Mr. Lathrop for opportunity and reaffirming my continuing interest in the firm in another capacity.

Maintain similar records as you network and conduct informational interviews. However, these cards will be classified differently and therefore should be kept together in a separate category called *"Networking"*. Organize these cards around the names of individuals. For example, at the top of a 4 x 6 card, place the name, address, and telephone number of your contact. Include any information which will clarify who this individual is in relationship to others and your job search. For example, this information might appear as follows:

TEMPLE, Joan (Mrs.)   1156 Terrace Dr., Richmond, VA 24810
                                        (703)212-8604

manager of Titan Corporation, security systems company. (see TITAN file info)

sister-in-law of John Graves. Received referral from John.

acquainted with Mary Cross, Dave Bairs, and Steve Rathing.

member of Grace Methodist church, Richmond Women's Network

graduate of the University of Virginia -- MBA, 1984. Classmate of Francis Catlin

sailing enthusiast

On the other side of this card, record all contact information. For example, you might include:

9/4/90   --   sent letter requesting informational interview via John Graves' recommendation

9/8/90   --   Made phone call; set luncheon appointment for 2/14

9/14/90   --   meeting; left resume; received 3 referrals -- Smith, David, Alton (see notes in STAPLES file)

9/15/90   --   sent thank-you letter

9/16/90   --   received phone call and 2 new referrals

9/18/90   --   received phone call and invitation to interview

---

You should also maintain active and inactive categories with both sets of cards. Keep the active file active by referring to each card once every two weeks. Make sure some activity has taken place between you and the contact within a four week period. This may mean sending another letter or telephoning the contact. If no new entries have been made on the card within eight weeks, move it to the inactive category. However, it is best to keep your contacts alive by continually monitoring contact dates and following-through with additional communication.

In addition to keeping an accurate set of 4 x 6 reference cards, be sure to keep all correspondence and notes in reference to your contact cards. This information can be best organized by using 9 x 12 file folders. Keep two sets of files. The first set should be organized by the names of contacts in your networking and informational interviewing campaigns. Copies of all correspondence coming to or from you should be included in these files. Also, include in each file all notes you take in reference to written communication, telephone, conversations, and interviews. Include a copy of the specific resume you sent or left with the individual. If you are using a general resume, note in your file folders which resume -- identified by coded number -- applies to the folder.

You may wish to take this record-keeping system one step further by developing a master record sheet. While this record sheet duplicates the information on your 4 x 6 cards and in your file folders, it provides you with a chronological listing of contact information. In abbreviated form, this information is much easier to carry with you than the cards and folders. It also enables you to quickly overview your campaign as well as evaluate your progress. Use our Master Record Sheet on page 192 for developing your own form.

This record-keeping system will enhance the effectiveness of your campaign. If you receive telephone calls in reference to your application or networking activities, you can immediately refer to the 4 x 6 cards and file folders during the course of your conversation. If not, you may find yourself in the embarrassing position of trying to remember whom you are talking to in reference to what. When writing additional correspondence, you will be able to quickly and accurately refer to previous communication.

Your record-keeping system will also allow you to *monitor and evaluate your progress.* These are important capabilities to develop throughout your job search. If, for example, after applying for 50 positions you are not invited to a single interview, re-evaluate your job search in reference to the published job market. Perhaps you are too aggressive or maybe you need to be more dramatic, such as sending copies of your

MASTER RECORD SHEET

Name/organization address	Telephone No.	Contact Source	Contact Dates				Active	Evaluation/Notes
			resume	letter	phone	interview		

resume on colored paper. Or perhaps you need to make greater use of the telephone to initiate interviews. Randomly select five companies from your inactive file of 50 and contact the employers; ask them for advice on how you might improve your campaign. This type of evaluation can result in some useful advice from those who manage the advertised job market. In addition, it may result in converting an inactive contact into an active networking contact.

You should periodically conduct a similar evaluation on your prospecting, networking, and informational interviewing campaign. Try to increase your efficiency and effectiveness by first analyzing your program and then taking corrective action. If your prospecting is not yielding contacts, re-structure your prospecting campaign. Your approach to people may need to be revised. Consider doing less letter writing and more telephone calling or alter your script for developing contacts. Your major problem may be in the number of contacts you initiate. Your probabilities of getting interviews and job offers will be in direct proportion to the number of prospects you develop and networks you maintain and expand. Your record-keeping system will give you an accurate picture of how diligent you have been in this regard. As your record-keeping system will confirm, you get results in direct proportion to the amount of time and effort you put into your job search.

THE ART OF ADVERTISING

Your job search campaign has similar characteristics to the art of advertising. Good advertisers know you must alter your advertising campaign if the number of responses do not justify your expenditure of time, effort, and money. While the product is sometimes defective or no demand can be created for it, more often than not the problem lies in how you position and market the product. Demands for products can usually be created if the product is clearly related to the needs and interests of the targeted audience and if the audience is continuously reminded that it is in their interests to acquire the product.

Results seldom occur overnight. Knowing how to effectively relate the product to the audience is often a trial and error process. Central to this process is a good record-keeping system which enables the advertiser to evaluate and adjust his or her campaign according to an improved understanding of one's particular audience.

Chapter Eleven

WELCOME OPPORTUNITIES

If you have carefully followed each of the preceding chapters, you should be well on your way to writing high impact resumes and letters for communicating your qualifications to employers. As we said from the very beginning, this type of written communication takes time and effort because it must be linked to other steps in the career planning and job search processes. The additional work involved should result in producing first class resumes and letters. If properly marketed, they should have a high probability of motivating employers to invite you to a job interview as well as generate referrals to other employers.

BUILDING ON FOUNDATIONS

If you decide to take the easy way out by editing our resume and letter examples, by all means study our models of the career planning and job search processes on pages 43 and 45. They stress a simple principle: *you should know where you are going before you get started.* You wouldn't take a major trip without a map or a guidebook, would you?

194

Writing resumes and letters without a basic foundational understanding of where you are coming from (skills and competencies) and where you are going (objective) is a sure way to conduct an aimless and ineffective job search. While you eventually will find some kind of job, you probably won't find a job that is *right for you.*

Communicating your objective and competencies in resumes and letters is the first step in developing high impact written communication. Knowing your audience also is important. You should target employers by conducting research on them. Conduct library research and talk to knowledgeable people.

Follow our principles, rules, and advice on developing form and content. But proper form and content are not enough. Your resume and letters must reach your intended audience. Connecting with the right people is possible if you prospect, network, and conduct informational interviews with your resume and letters. In so doing, you will open doors by communicating that you are purposeful and competent. You should demonstrate your value by emphasizing what you can do well.

YOUR NEXT STEPS

While this book takes you through most career planning steps, it does not direct you through the final two steps -- interviewing and negotiating the job offer. These are subjects of other books. Formal interviews and negotiations come *after* you achieve initial impact. Prepare for these critical steps like you organize your resume and letters -- with purpose and thoroughness.

Finding a job that is right for you will take time, patience, and hard work. Our principles for achieving a successful job search (pages 61-64) are especially important for *implementation and follow-through.* If you have difficulty in this regard, develop a job search management scheme as outlined in Chapter Five; find someone to monitor your daily progress.

OPTIMISM WITH PRAGMATISM

Regardless of what others tell you, it is not easy to find a job that is right for you. It requires work. For some people, this may be the hardest work they ever do! Surely it is one of the most important activities of your career.

The job search becomes difficult because of its very personal and ego involved nature. You lay your ego on the line when you apply for a position, ask for employment assistance, or interview for a job. You condense years of experience and value into a one or two-page resume. When you conduct the job search, you open important aspects of your life to total strangers.

But rejections are part of the job search game. You will likely receive several rejections before you get the acceptances that count -- an interview and job offer. The best way to handle rejections is to:

- Recognize your value as going beyond immediate job search situations.

- Practice marketing techniques that minimize the number of rejections you might receive, such as networking.

- Don't become too ego involved by taking yourself and each up and down in the job search too seriously.

- Remember the probabilistic nature of any job search.

- Keep busy by moving on to new job leads, networking, and following-up, In other words, it may not be good to think too much about any one job search situation.

We recommend an optimistic/pragmatic job search perspective. In part, you are playing a *probability game* where the outcomes are similar to the combinations of apples and oranges that come up in a slot machine. The longer you keep at it, the more rejections -- and acceptances -- you are likely to encounter. However, unlike the casino, luck is only a part of the equation. The greater the quality and effort you put into your job search, the more you are likely to get out of it.

Employers look for a special *"fit"*, but you may not fit at a particular time and in a particular place. Like the slot machine, the right combination of apples and oranges will come up as long as you keep at it. While persistence and patience will pay off, a well planned job search with high impact resumes and letters should increase your probabilities of success.

LUCK COMES YOUR WAY

We hope you will avoid the many pitfalls and emotional thumps other job seekers experience. Writing high impact resumes and letters will get you off to a good start and prepare you for the other job search steps.

Luck will come your way if you prepare to seize opportunities. Good luck and enjoy your job search. Whatever you do, make sure you give it direction with high impact resumes and letters.

Chapter Twelve

CAREER AND JOB SEARCH RESOURCES

During the past 20 years hundreds of self-help books have been written on how to find a job and advance one's career. Each year dozens of additional volumes are published to inform as well as enlighten a growing audience of individuals concerned with conducting an effective job search. Many of these books focus on writing effective resumes and letters.

In this chapter we attempt to bring some coherence and organization to this literature for identifying additional resources. If *High Impact Resumes and Letters* is your first job search book, you may find many of our recommendations in this section useful for organizing your other job search activities. Since many of these books are difficult to find in local bookstores or libraries, you may need to order them directly from the publishers. For your convenience, you can order most of the books through *Impact Publications* by completing the order form at the end of this book. For a more complete listing of career planning and job search resources, contact our publisher to receive a free copy of their annotated catalog of nearly 1,000 resources. See pages 5-6 for ordering details.

CHOOSING WHAT'S BEST FOR YOU

You may be initially overwhelmed with the sheer volume of the career planning and job search literature available to help individuals find jobs and change careers. Once you examine a few books, such as this one, you will quickly learn that this literature is designed to be *used*. The books are not designed to describe a subject, explain reality, develop a theory, nor predict the future.

Most career planning and job search books attempt to *advance self-help strategies* based upon the particular ideas or experiences of individual writers. They expound a *set of beliefs* -- more or less logical and based on a mixture of research, experience, and faith. Like other how-to literature on achieving success, you must first *believe* in these books before you can make them work for you. Since the research base for most of these books is very thin, this literature must be primarily judged on the basis of faith and usefulness.

Given the nature of this literature, your best approach is to *pick and choose* which books are *more or less useful* for you. There is nothing magical about these books. At best, they may challenge your preconceptions; develop alternative beliefs which you may or may not find acceptable; provide you with some directions; and help motivate you to implement an effective job search. They will not get you a job.

The level of redundancy in this literature may be disturbing to many readers. Moreso than in many other fields, career planning writers tend to quote each other or rely on the perspectives of a few key writers in restating the same approaches in a different form. As a result, many individuals confuse the high level of redundancy as repeated evidence of career and job search *"facts"*.

WHAT YOU GET

We have examined most of the career planning and job search literature with a view toward identifying the best of the lot. We've judged the literature in terms of its degree of accuracy, realism, comprehensiveness, and usefulness. In doing so, we have found three major types of books which use different approaches to getting a job:

- Books designed to teach key job search *process and strategy skills*; these books emphasize *"how"* questions.

- Books designed to outline various *employment fields*; these books focus on *"what"* and *"where"* questions.

- Books designed to address key career issues for *special groups*; these books emphasize *"what"* and *"how"* questions.

A growing number of comprehensive job search books attempt to apply the process and strategy skills to different employment fields and special groups.

PROCESS AND STRATEGY SKILLS

The first type of career planning and job search literature concentrates primarily on developing *process and strategy skills*. Most of these books tell you *how* to develop an effective job search regardless of your particular employment field or your specialized needs. They seldom address substantive *what* and *where* questions central to finding any job. You are left to answer these questions on your own or by using other resources which focus on what jobs are available and where you can find them.

There are no surprises in this literature since most of the books follow a similar pattern in approaching the subject. The major difference is that the books are more or less readable. Most of these process books are preoccupied with *"getting in touch with yourself"* by emphasizing the need to *"know what you want to do today, tomorrow, and the rest of your life."* Some of this literature is rightly referred to as *"touchy-feely"* because of its concern with trying to get you to know yourself -- the basis for self-assessment. A mainstay of psychologists, counselors, and activity-oriented trainers, this type of positive, up-beat literature is at best designed to reorient your life around (1) identifying what is right about yourself (*your strengths*), and (2) setting goals based upon an understanding of your past and present in the hope you will do better in the future (*your objectives*).

The real strengths of this literature lie in orienting your thinking along new lines, providing you with some baseline information on your strengths and goals, and providing you with positive motivation for developing and implementing an effective job search strategy. If you're looking for specifics, such as learning *what* the jobs are and *where* you can find them, this literature may disappoint you with its vagueness.

Placed within our career planning framework in Chapter Four, much of this process and strategy literature falls into the initial two steps of our career planning process: self-assessment and objective setting. Examples of career planning literature using this approach are the popular books written by Bolles, Crystal, Miller, Mattson, Sher, and Krannich: *Where Do I Go From Here With My Life?*, *What Color Is Your Parachute?*, *The Three Boxes of Life*, *The Truth About You*, *Wishcraft*, and *Discover the Right Job for You!* You should read these books if you lack a clear understanding of who you are, what you want to do, and where you are going. They may help you get in touch with yourself before you get in touch with employers! If these self-discovery books don't deliver with such self-understanding, you probably need to see a professional counselor who can administer tests as well as walk you through a comprehensive self-assessment process.

Several books focus on additional steps in the career planning and job search processes, such as doing research, writing resumes and letters, networking, interviewing, and negotiating salary. While also emphasizing process and strategy, these are more comprehensive books than the others. Some books include all of the job search steps whereas others concentrate on one or two major steps. Examples of the most comprehensive such books include those written by Krannich, Kennedy and Laramore, Hecklinger and Curtin, Lathrop, Jackson, Figler, Irish, Snelling, and Studner: *Careering and Re-Careering For the 1990s*, *Joyce Lain Kennedy's Career Book*, *Training For Life*, *Who's Hiring Who*, *The Complete Job Search Handbook*, *Guerrilla Tactics in the Job Market*, *Go Hire Yourself an Employer*, *The Right Job*, and *Super Job Search*.

You will find hundreds of books that focus on the *research stage* of the job search. Most of these books are geographic, field, or organizational directories or job banks which list names and addresses of potential employers. Examples include the Bob Adams' *Job Bank Series* on 17 major cities and metropolitan areas, Surrey Book's *How To Get a Job in...* series on nine cities, Wright's *The American Almanac of Jobs and Salaries*, Schwartz's and Brechner's *The Career Finder*, Plunkett's *The Almanac of American Employers*, Levering's *100 Best Companies To Work For in America*, Krantz's *The Jobs Rated Almanac*, Berreto's *California: Where to Work, Where to Live*, Levine's *Corporate Address Book*, Lauber's *The Compleat Guide to Finding Jobs in Government*, and Dun and Bradstreet's *The Career Guide: Dun's Employment Opportunity Directory*. Job search approaches relating to much of this literature are in sharp contrast to approaches of the standard career planning literature. Directories, for example, should be used to gather information -- names, addresses, and phone numbers -- to be used in targeting one's networking activities rather than as sources for shotgunning resumes and letters.

Numerous books are written on other key job search steps -- especially resume and letter writing and job interviews. The *resume and letter writing* books fall into two major categories:

- Books designed to walk you through the process of developing a resume based upon a thorough understanding of each step in the job search process. Examples include Krannich's and Banis' *High Impact Resumes and Letters*, Jackson's *The Perfect Resume*, Fry's *Your First Resume*, and Good's *Does Your Resume Wear Blue Jeans?*

- Books primarily presenting examples of resumes and letters. Examples of such books are numerous -- most resume books you will find in libraries and bookstores fall in this category. One of the best such books is Parker's *The Resume Catalog*.

The first type of resume and letter writing book urges the user to develop resumes and letters that represent the *"unique you"* in relation to specific positions and employers. They further emphasize the importance of finding a job that is right for you rather than try to adjust your experience to fit into a job that may be inappropriate for you. These books are based upon a particular approach to finding a job as outlined in several of the comprehensive career planning and job search books.

The second type of resume and letter writing book lacks a clear approach other than an implied suggestion that readers should creatively plagiarize the examples. In other words, good resumes and letters are produced by osmosis! A few resume and letter writing books, such as Parker's *The Damn Good Resume Guide*, Schuman's and Lewis' *Revising Your Resume*, Yate's *Resumes That Knock 'Em Dead*, and Beatty's *The Perfect Cover Letter* fall between these two types.

Several books address the issue of *networking* in the job search. Most of these books, however, focus on formal organizations or groups and communication networks relevant to womens' issues rather than on networks and the process of networking in the job search. Examples include Kleiman's *Women's Networks* and Stern's *Is Networking For You?* While several job search books include a short section on networking -- discuss the importance of networking and give a few examples of networks and networking -- the Krannichs' *Network Your Way To Job and Career Success* is the only book to focus solely in the role of networking in the job search process. Boe and Youngs' *Is Your "Net" Working?* looks at how to build contacts for career development.

You will also find several *job interview* books designed for both interviewees and interviewers. Most of these books examine each step in the interview process -- from preparation to negotiating salary. Interview books such as the Krannichs' *Interview For Success* look at each step of the interview process within a well defined career development and job search process. Some interview books, such as Yate's *Knock 'Em Dead* and Allen's *The Complete Q & A Job Interview Book*, focus primarily on questions and answers. Other interview books are more comprehensive, including interview settings, types of interviews, and nonverbal communication along with a discussion of appropriate questions and answers. Some of the better interview books are written by Vlk, Meyer and Berchtold, Elderkin, and Medley: *Interviews That Get Results*, *Getting the Job: How To Interview Successfully*, *How to Interviews From Job Ads*, and *Sweaty Palms*.

While most comprehensive job search and interview books include a section on salary negotiations, a few books have been written specifically on this subject. However, most of these books are now out of print, but they may be available in your local library. Examples include Kennedy's *Salary Strategies* and Chastain's *Winning the Salary Game*. The Krannichs' new *Salary Success: Know What You're Worth and Get It!* examines both salary negotiation strategies as well as data on salary ranges for specific occupations and jobs. Much of the general literature on negotiation tactics is relevant to this topic.

SPECIFIC EMPLOYMENT FIELDS

A second type of career and job search literature focuses primarily on specific employment fields. These books come in many forms. Some are designed to give the reader a general overview of what type of work is involved in each field. Other books include educational training and job search strategies appropriate for entry into each field. And still others are annotated listings of job and career titles -- the most comprehensive being the Department of Labor's *Occupational Outlook Handbook* and *The Dictionary of Occupational Titles*.

The majority of books on employment fields are designed for individuals who are considering a particular employment field rather than for individuals wishing to advance within a field. As such, most of these books are general introductions designed to answer important *"what"*, *"where"*, and *"how"* questions for high school and college students. They provide little useful information for older and more experienced professionals who need more detailed and advanced information on their specific employment field. Examples of such books include the 125 volumes in National Textbook's *Opportunities in... Series* with such titles as *Opportunities in Architecture, Opportunities in Office Occupations, Opportunities in Public Relations, Opportunities in Forestry*, and *Opportunities in Travel Careers*. More and more books are being produced in specific employment fields, especially for computer, business, accounting, medical, government, international, communication, media, and travel specialists.

SPECIALIZED CAREER GROUPS

A final set of career planning and job search books has emerged during the past few years. These books are designed for specific groups of job seekers who supposedly need specialized assistance not found in most general job search process and employment field books. The most common such books focus on women, minorities, the handicapped, immigrants, public employees, military personnel, educators, mobile spouses, college graduates, children, and teenagers.

Many of these books represent a new type of career planning book that has emerged during the past few years and will most likely continue in the foreseeable future. Several books deal with both *process* and *substance*. They link the substantive *"what"* and *"where"* concerns of specific employment fields to *"how"* processes appropriately outlined for each field.

Take, for example, the field of advertising. Several new books, such as Caffrey's *So You Want to Be in Advertising*, Mogal's *Making it in the Media Professions*, and Fry's *The Advertising Career Directory* now outline the jobs available in the field of advertising (*what questions*); where you should look for vacancies (*where questions*); and the best strategies for finding a job, including resumes, letters, and interview questions appropriate for the advertising field (*how questions*).

These specialized career books finally identify how general job search strategies must be adapted and modified to respond to the employment needs of different types of individuals as well as to the employment cultures found in different fields. Some of the most popular such books include *The Black Woman's Career Guide, Job Hunting For the Disabled, Getting a Job In the United States, The Complete Guide To Public Employment, The Complete Guide to International Jobs and Careers, From the Military To a Civilian Career, Moving Out of Education, Alternative Careers for Teachers, The Relocating Spouse's Guide To Employment,*

Liberal Arts Jobs, and *Summer Opportunities For Kids and Teenagers*.

In the coming decade we can expect to see many more career planning books produced along these combined process, field, and specialized group lines. While general career planning books focusing only on process and strategy will continue to proliferate, the real excitement in this field will be centered around the continuing development of books which link the job search and career planning processes to specific employment fields and specialized groups. If, for example, you are in the fields of real estate or robotics, you should be able to find books outlining what the jobs are, where to find them, and how to get them. Such books will most likely be written by seasoned professionals who represent specialized groups rather than by career planning professionals who are primarily trained in process skills. Such books will meet a growing need for information from individuals who have a solid understanding of how to get a job based on familiarity with the *"ins"* and *"outs"* of each field.

The following bibliography includes some of the best career planning books available today. Consistent with the structure of this book and our discussion of career planning and job search literature, we have organized the bibliography according to process, field, and group categories.

BIBLIOGRAPHY

Job Search Strategies and Tactics

Figler, Howard E., *The Complete Job Search Handbook* (New York: Holt, Rinehart, and Winston, 1988)

Hecklinger, Fred J. and Bernadette M. Curtin, *Training For Life: A Practical Guide To Career and Life Planning* (Dubuque, IA: Kendell/Hunt Publishing, 1988).

Irish, Richard K., *Go Hire Yourself An Employer* (New York: Doubleday, 1987).

Jackson, Tom, *Guerrilla Tactics in the Job Market* (New York: Bantam, 1980).

Kennedy, Joyce Lain and Darryl Laramore, *The Joyce Lain Kennedy's Career Book* (Lincolnwood, IL: National Textbook, 1988).

Krannich, Ronald L., *Careering and Re-Careering For the 1990s* (Manassas, VA: Impact Publications, 1989).

Lathrop, Richard, *Who's Hiring Who* (Berkeley, CA: Ten Speed Press, 1989).

Rogers, Edward J., *Getting Hired* (Englewood, NJ: Prentice Hall, 1982).

Sher, Barbara, *Wishcraft: How To Get What You Really Want* (New York: Ballantine, 1983).

Snelling, Sr., Robert O., *The Right Job* (New York: Viking Penguin, 1987).

Stanat, Kirby W., *Job Hunting Secrets & Tactics* (Piscataway, NJ: New Century Publishers, 1977).

Studner, Peter K., *Super Job Search* (Los Angeles, CA: Jamenair Ltd., 1987).

Wegmann, Robert, Robert Chapman, and Miriam Johnson, *Work in the New Economy* (Indianapolis, IN: JIST Works, 1989).

Skills Identification, Testing, and Self-Assessment

Bolles, Richard N., *The New Quick Job Hunting Map* (Berkeley, CA: Ten Speed Press, 1985).

Bolles, Richard N., *The Three Boxes of Life* (Berkeley, CA: Ten Speed Press, 1981).

Bolles, Richard N., *What Color Is Your Parachute?* (Berkeley, CA: Ten Speed Press, 1990).

Branden, Nathaniel, *How To Raise Your Self-Esteem* (New York: Bantam, 1986).

Crystal, John C. and Richard N. Bolles, *Where Do I Go From Here With My Life?* (Berkeley, CA: Ten Speed Press, 1979).

Dahl, Dan and Randolph Sykes, *Charting Your Goals* (New York: Harper and Row, 1988).

Gale, Barry and Linda Gale, *Discover What You're Best At* (New York: Simon & Schuster, 1983).

Holland, John L., *Making Vocational Choices* (Englewood Cliffs, NJ: Prentice-Hall, 1985).

Miller, Arthur F. and Ralph T. Mattson, *The Truth About You: Discover What You Should Be Doing With Your Life* (Berkeley, CA: Ten Speed Press, 1989).

Moskowitz, Robert, *How To Organize Your Work and Your Life* (New York: Doubleday, 1981).

Krannich, Ronald L. and Caryl Rae, *Discover the Right Job for You!* (Manassas, VA: Impact Publications, 1990).

Scheele, Adele, *Skills For Success* (New York: Ballantine, 1979).

Research on Cities, Fields, and Organizations

Adams Inc., Bob (ed.), *The Job Bank Series: Atlanta, Boston, Chicago, Dallas, Denver, Detroit, Florida, Houston, Los Angeles, Minneapolis, New York, Ohio, Philadelphia, San Francisco, Seattle, St. Louis, Washington, DC* (Boston, MA: Bob Adams, Inc., 1988-1990).

Adams Inc., Bob (ed.), *The National Job Bank* (Boston, MA: Bob Adams, Inc., 1990).

Berreto, Helena, *California: Where to Work, Where to Live* (Rocklin, CA: Prima Publishing and Communications, 1989.

Camden, Bishop, Schwartz, Greene, Fleming-Holland, *"How To Get a Job in..." Insider's City Guides: Atlanta, Chicago, Dallas/Ft. Worth, Houston, Los Angeles/San Diego, New York, San Francisco, Seattle/Portland, Washington, DC* (Chicago, IL: Surrey, 1989-1990).

Career Associates, *Career Choices: Art, Business, Communications and Journalism, Computer Science, Economics, English, History, Law, Mathematics, MBA, Political Science and Government, Psychology* (New York: Walker and Co., 1990).

Career Associates, *Career Choices Encyclopedia* (New York: Walker and Co., 1989).

Career Press, *The Career Directory Series: Advertising, Book Publishing, Business and Finance, Magazine Publishing, Marketing, Newspaper Publishing, Public Relations, Travel and Hospitality* (Hawthorne, NJ: The Career Press, 1990).

Hopke, William (ed.), *Encyclopedia of Careers and Vocational Guidance* (Chicago, IL: J. G. Ferguson, 1987).

Krantz, Less, *The Jobs Rated Almanac* (New York: Pharos Books, 1988).

Levering, Robert, Milton Moskowitz, and Michael Katz, *The 100 Best Companies To Work For In America* (Chicago, IL: NAL, 1985).

Norback, Craig T., *Careers Encyclopedia* (Lincolnwood, IL: National Textbook, 1988).

Plunkett, Jack W., *The Almanac of American Employers* (Chicago, IL: Contemporary Books, 1985).

Schwartz, Lester and Irv Brechner, *The Career Finder* (New York: Ballantine, 1982).

U.S. Department of Labor, *The Occupational Outlook Handbook* (Washington, DC: U.S. Department of Labor, 1990).

Wright, John W., *The American Almanac of Jobs and Salaries* (New York: Avon, 1987).

Resumes and Letters

Beatty, Richard H., *The Perfect Cover Letter* (New York: Wiley, 1989).

Bostwick, Burdette E., *Resume Writing* (New York: Wiley, 1984).

Fry, Ronald W., *Your First Resume* (Hawthorne, NJ: Career Press, 1989).

Good, C. Edward, *Does Your Resume Wear Apron Strings?* (Charlottesville, VA: Blue Jeans Press, 1989).

Good, C. Edward, *Does Your Resume Wear Blue Jeans?* (Charlottesville, VA: Blue Jeans Press, 1985).

Jackson, Tom, *The Perfect Resume* (New York: Doubleday, 1981).

Krannich, Ronald L. and William Banis, *High Impact Resumes and Letters* (Woodbridge, VA: Impact Publications, 1990).

Parker, Yana, *The Damn Good Resume Guide* (Berkeley, NY: Ten Speed Press, 1986).

Parker, Yana, *The Resume Catalog* (Berkeley, NY: Ten Speed Press, 1988).

Schuman, Nancy and William Lewis, *Revising Your Resume* (New York: Wiley, 1987).

Yate, Martin John, *Resumes That Knock 'Em Dead* (Holbrook, MA: Bob Adams, 1988).

Networking

Boe, Anne and Bettie B. Youngs, *Is Your "Net" Working?* (New York: Wiley, 1989).

Kleiman, Carol, *Women's Networks* (New York: Ballantine, 1982).

Krannich, Ronald L. and Caryl Rae Krannich, *Network Your Way To Job and Career Success* (Manassas, VA: Impact Publications, 1989).

Dress, Appearance, and Image

Bixler, Susan, *The Professional Image* (New York: Putnam,1984).

Jackson, Carole, *Color Me Beautiful* (Washington, DC: Acropolis, 1986).

Karpinski, Kenneth J., *The Winner's Style* (Washington, DC: Acropolis Press, 1987).

Martin, Judith, *Miss Manners' Guide to the Turn-of-the Millennium* (New York: St. Martin's Press, 1989)

Molloy, John T., *Dress For Success* (New York: Warner, 1988).

Molloy, John T., *The Woman's Dress For Success Book* (New York: Warner, 1977).

Nicholson, JoAnne and Judy Lewis-Crum, *Color Wonderful* (New York: Bantam, 1986).

Wallach, Janet, *Working Wardrobe* (New York: Warner, 1981).

Interviews and Salary Negotiations

Beatty, R. H., *The Five Minute Interview* (New York: Wiley, 1986).

Chapman, Jack, *How To Make $1000 A Minute: Negotiating Salaries and Raises* (Berkeley, CA: Ten Speed Press, 1987).

Chastain, Sherry, *Winning the Salary Game* (New York: Wiley, 1980).

Kennedy, Marilyn Moats, *Salary Strategies* (New York: Scribners, 1982).

Krannich, Caryl Rae and Ronald L. Krannich, *Interview For Success* (Woodbridge, VA: Impact Publications, 1990).

Krannich, Ronald L. and Caryl Rae Krannich, *Salary Success* (Woodbridge, VA: Impact Publications, 1990).

Medley, H. Anthony, *Sweaty Palms* (Berkeley, CA: Ten Speed Press, 1984).

Meyer, Mary Coeli and Inge M. Berchtold, *Getting the Job: How to Interview Successfully* (Princeton, NJ: Petrocelli, 1982).

Vlk, Suzee, *Interviews That Get Results* (New York: Simon & Schuster, 1984).

Yate, Martin John, *Knock 'Em Dead With Great Answers to Tough Interview Questions* (Boston, MA: Bob Adams, Inc., 1986).

Educators

Bastress, Fran, *Teachers In New Careers* (Cranston, RI: Carroll Press, 1984).

Krannich, Ronald L. and William Banis, *Moving Out of Education* (Manasssas, VA: Impact Publications, 1985).

Pollack, Sandy, *Alternative Careers For Teachers* (Boston, MA: Harvard Common Press, 1986).

Public-Oriented Careers

Krannich, Ronald L. and Caryl Rae Krannich, *The Complete Guide to Public Employment* (Woodbridge, VA: Impact Publications, 1990).

Krannich, Ronald L. and Caryl Rae Krannich, *Find a Federal Job Fast!* (Woodbridge, VA: Impact Publications, 1990).

Lauber, Daniel, *The Compleat Guide To Finding Jobs in Government* (Evanston, IL: Planning/Communications, 1989).

McAdams, Terry W., *Careers In the Nonprofit Sector* (Washington, DC: The Taft Group, 1986).

Phillips, David Atlee, *Careers in Secret Operations* (Bethesda, MD: Stone Trail Press, 1984).

Waelde, David E., *How To Get a Federal Job* (Washington, DC: FED-HELP, 1989).

Wood, Patricia B., *The 171 Reference Book* (Washington, DC: Workbooks, Inc., 1986).

International and Overseas Jobs

Beckmann, David M., Timothy J. Mitchell, and Linda L. Powers, *The Overseas List* (Minneapolis, MN: Augsburg Publishing, 1986).

Cantrell, Will and Terry Marshall, *101 Ways To Find an Overseas Job* (McLean, VA: Cantrell Corporation, 1987).

Casewit, Curtis W., *How To Get a Job Overseas* (New York: Prentice-Hall, 1984).

Foreign Policy Association (ed.), *Guide To Careers in World Affairs* (New York: Foreign Policy Association, 1987).

Kocher, Eric, *International Jobs* (Reading, MA: Addison-Wesley, 1989).

Krannich, Ronald L. and Caryl Rae Krannich, *The Complete Guide to International Jobs and Careers* (Woodbridge, VA: Impact Publications, 1990).

Powers, Linda (ed.), *Careers In International Affairs* (Washington, DC: Georgetown University School of Foreign Service, 1986).

Win, David, *International Careers: An Insider's Guide* (Charlotte, VT: Williamson Publishing, 1987).

Military

Bradley, Jeff, *A Young Person's Guide To the Military* (Boston, MA: Harvard Common Press, 1987).

Garlock, Michael, *From Soldier To Civilian* (New York: Prentice-Hall, 1988).

Marrs, Texe and Karen Read, *The Woman's Guide To Military Service* (Cockeysville, MD: Liberty Publishing, 1986).

Nyman, Keith O., *Re-Entry: Turning Military Experience Into Civilian Success* (Harrisonburg, PA: Stackpole Books, 1990).

Petit, Ron, *From the Military To a Civilian Career* (Harrisonburg, VA: Maron Publications, 1984).

Women and Spouses

Bastress, Fran, *The Relocating Spouse's Guide To Employment* (Chevy Chase, MD: Woodley Publications, 1989).

Catalyst, *What To Do With the Rest of Your Life* (New York: Simon & Schuster, 1980).

Lewis, William and Nancy Schuman, *Back To Work: A Career Guide For the Returnee* (Woodbury, NY: Barron's, 1985).

Nivens, Beatryce, *Careers For Women Without College Degrees* (New York: McGraw-Hill, 1988).

Zeitz, Daila and Lorraine Dusky, *The Best Companies For Women* (New York: Simon & Schuster, 1988).

College Students

Career Associates, *"Career Choices in..." Series: Art, Business, Communications and Journalism, Computer Science, Economics, English, History, Law, Mathematics, MBA, Political Science and Government,* and *Psychology.*

Falvey, Jack, *After College: The Business of Getting Jobs* (Charlotte, VT: Williamson Publishing, 1986).

Fox, Marcia R., *Put Your Degree To Work* (New York: W. W. Norton, 1988).

LaFevre, John L., *How You Really Get Hired* (New York: Simon & Schuster, 1989).

Lento-McGovern, Diane, *Life After College: Which Direction Is Best For You?* (White Hall, VA: Betterway Publications, 1986).

Munschauer, John L., *Jobs For English Majors and Other Smart People* (Princeton, NJ: Peterson's Guides, 1986).

Nadler, Burton Jay, *Liberal Arts Jobs* (Princeton, NJ: Peterson's Guides, 1985).

Phifer, Paul, *College Majors and Careers* (Garrett Park, MD: Garrett Park Press, 1987).

Reyes-Guerra, David R. and Allan M. Fischer, *The Engineering/High-Tech Student's Handbook* (Princeton, NJ: Peterson's Guides, 1990).

Salzman, Marian and Nancy Marx Better, *Wanted: Liberal Arts Graduates* (New York: Doubleday, 1987).

Children, Youth, and Summer Jobs

Billy, Christopher (ed.), *Summer Opportunities For Kids and Teenagers* (Princeton, NJ: Peterson's Guides, 1990).

Catalyst, *It's Your Future: Catalyst's Career Guide For High School Girls* (Princeton, NJ: Peterson's Guides, 1982).

Children's Dictionary of Occupations (Bloomington, IL: Meridian Educational Corp., 1985).

Douglas, Martha, *Go For It!* (Berkeley, CA: Ten Speed Press, 1983).

Greenberg, Jan W., *The Teenager's Guide to the Best Summer Opportunities* (Boston, MA: Harvard Common Press, 1985).

Lee, Rose P., *A Real Job For You: An Employment Guide For Teens* (White Hall, VA: Betterway Publications, 1984).

Minorities, Immigrants, and Disabled

Friedenberg, Joan E. and Curtis H. Bradley, *Finding a Job In the United States* (Lincolnwood, IL: National Textbook, 1986).

Johnson, Willis L. (ed.), *Directory of Special Programs For Minority Group Members* (Garrett Park, MD: Garrett Park Press, 1990).

Lewis, Adele and Edith Marks, *Job Hunting For the Disabled* (Woodbury, NY: Barron's, 1983).

Nivens, Beatryce, *The Black Woman's Career Guide* (New York: Doubleday, 1987).

Experienced and Elderly

Birsner, E. Patricia, *The 40+ Job Hunting Guide* (New York: Prentice-Hall, 1986).

Falvey, Jack, *What's Next? Career Strategies After 35* (Charlotte, VT: Williamson Publishing, 1986).

Morgan, John S., *Getting a Job After 50* (Blue Ridge Summit,PA: TAB Books, 1987).

Myers, Albert and Christopher Anderson, *Success Over Sixty* (New York: Simon & Schuster, 1986).

Alternative Career Fields

Billy, Christopher (ed.), *Business and Management Jobs* (Princeton, NJ: Peterson's Guides, 1990).

Billy, Christopher (ed.), *Engineering, Science, and Computer Jobs* (Princeton, NJ: Peterson's Guides, 1990).

Boyd, Wilma, *Travel Agent* (New York: Arco, 1989).

Cordoza, Anne and Suzee J. Vlk, *The Aerospace Career Handbook* (New York: Arco, 1984).

Cordoza, Anne and Suzee J. Vlk, *The Robotics Career Handbook* (New York: Arco, 1984).

Edward, Kenneth W., *Your Successful Real Estate Career* (New York: AMACOM, 1987).

Field, Shelly, *Career Opportunities In the Music Industry* (New York: Facts on File, 1986).

Hawes, Gene R. and Douglas L. Brownstone, *The Outdoor Careers Guide* New York: Facts on File, 1986).

Mogel, Leonard, *Making It in the Media Professions* (Chester, CT: The Globe Pequot Press, 1988).

New Accountant Co., *New Accountant Careers* (Glen Cove, NY: New Accountant Co., 1989).

"Opportunities in..." Career Series (125 titles), (Lincolnwood, IL: National Textbook, 1984-1990).

Rubin, K., *Flying High In Travel: A Complete Guide To Careers In the Travel Industry* (New York: Wiley, 1986).

Rucker, T. Donald and Martin D. Keller, *Planning Your Medical Career* (Garrett Park, MD: Garrett Park Press, 1987).

Appendix A

RESUME TRANSFORMATIONS

The following examples represent an actual case study. While it is not a typical case, it does emphasize some important employment problems which can be handled with different types of resumes. The individual held several full-time positions as typist, secretary, receptionist, and sales clerk while working her way through college. After graduation, she continued in her former occupation. Wanting to break out of the *"once a secretary, always a secretary"* pattern, she has several resume options for changing careers. Everything appearing in these resumes is *true*. One of the major differences is the truth is better communicated in some resumes than in others.

The first resume represents the **traditional chronological or "obituary" resume**. It stresses skills and accomplishments in relationship to an objective. In this resume, the individual presents those jobs which strengthen her objective.

The *functional resume* on page 219 presents another picture of this individual's qualifications. Here, employment dates and job titles are eliminated in favor of presenting transferable skills and accomplishments. While this resume is ideal for someone entering the job market with little job related experience, this resume does not take advantage of this individual's work experience with specific employers.

The *combination resume* on page 220 is ideal for this particular person. It minimizes employment dates and job titles, stresses transferable skills and accomplishments, and includes work history. The individual appears purposeful, skilled, and experienced.

The resume letter on page 221 also is a good alternative for this person. It is designed to open doors without the traditional resume. The individual can present one of the resumes -- preferably the combination resume -- to the employer at some later date.

The secretarial experience does not appear on the chronological, functional, or combination resumes. If it did, it would tend to stereotype this individual prior to being invited to an interview. It is important, however, that this individual be able to explain the secretarial experience during the interview, especially how it will make her a particularly good salesperson -- knows the particular equipment and problems from the perspective of those who will use it on a day-to-day basis.

Traditional Chronological Resume

RESUME

Gail S. Topper   Weight: 122 lbs.
136 W. Davis St.   Height: 5'4"
Washington, DC 20030   Born: August 4, 1954
202-465-9821   Health: Good
                                                    Marital Status: Married

Education

1984-1986   University of Maryland. College Park, Maryland.
             I worked toward my M.A. in English.

1980-1983   George Mason University. Fairfax, Virginia.
             I received my B.A. in Communication.

1977-1979   Northern Virginia Community College, Annandale,
             Virginia, I completed my A.A. degree.

1972-1976   Harrisonburg High School. Harrisonburg, Virginia.

Work Experience

2/14/86 to present: Secretary. MCT Corporation, 2381 Rhode Island
             Ave., S.W., Washington, D.C. 20033.

2/30/84 to 2/9/86: Secretary, Martin Computer Services, 391 Old
             Dominion Rd., Annandale, Virginia 20789.

4/21/83 to 2/20/84: Secretary, STR Systems, Inc., 442 Virginia Ave.,
             Rm. 21, Washington, D.C. 20011.

9/28/82 to 1/4/83: Typist, NTC Corporation, 992 Fairy Avenue,
             Springfield, Virginia 22451.

3/1/80 to 9/14/82: Salesclerk, Sears Roebuck & Co., 294 Wisconsin
             Avenue, Washington, D.C. 20013.

5/3/77 to 2/1/79: Salesclerk, JT's, 332 Monroe St., Washington, D.C.
             20014.

1972-1976:   held several jobs as cook, counter help, salesclerk, typist,
             and secretarial assistant.

Community Involvement

1984 to present: Sunday school teacher. Grace Methodist Church.
             Falls Church, Virginia.

1983:   Volunteer. Red Cross. Falls Church, Virginia.

1979: Stage crew member. Community Theatre Group. Annandale, Virginia.

1978: Extra. Community Theatre Group. Annandale, Virginia.

Hobbies

I like to swim, cook, garden, bicycle, and listen to rock music.

Personal Statement

I have good mannual dexterity developed by working back stage in theatrical productions and working with various office machines. I can operate IBM Mag Card A and II typewriters, dictaphones, IBM 6640 (ink jet printer), various duplicating machines, and several copying machines. Familiar with addressograph. I am willing to relocate and travel.

References

John R. Teems, Manager, Martin Computer Services, 391 Old Dominion Rd., Annandale, Virginia 20789.

Jane Stevens, Secretary, STR Systems, Inc., 442 Virginia Ave., Rm. 21, Washington, D.C. 20011.

Alice Bears, Assistant Personnel Director, MCT Corporation, 2381 Rhode Island Ave., Washington, D.C. 20033.

Also contact the Office of Career Planning and Placement at George Mason University.

Chronological Resume

———————— GAIL S. TOPPER ————————

136 West Davis Street
Washington, D.C. 20030   202/465-9821

OBJECTIVE: A professional sales position. . . leading to management. . . in information processing where administrative
and technical experience, initiative, and interpersonal skills
will be utilized for maximizing sales and promoting good
customer relations.

EDUCATION: B.A. in Communication, 1983
George Mason University, Fairfax, Virginia.

- Courses in interpersonal communication, psychology,
  and public speaking.
- Worked full-time in earning 100% of educational and
  personal expenses.

TECHNICAL   MCT Corporation, 2381 Rhode Island Ave., S.W.,
EXPERIENCE: Washington, D.C. 20033: Office management and materials production responsibilities. Planned and re-organized
word processing center. Initiated time and cost studies,
which saved company $30,000 in additional labor costs.
Improved efficiency of personnel. 1986 to present.

Martin Computer Services, 391 Old Dominion Rd.,
Annandale, Virginia 20789: Communication and
materials production responsibilities. Handled customer
complaints. Created new tracking and filing system for
Mag cards. Improved turnaround time for documents
production. Operated Savin word processor. 1984 to 1986.

STR Systems, 442 Virginia Avenue, Rm. 21, Washington, D.C. 20011: Equipment operation and production
responsibilities. Operated Mag card and high speed printers:
IBM 6240, Mag A, I, II, IBM 6640. Developed and organized
technical reference room for more effective use of equipment.
1983-1984.

SALES   Sears Roebuck & Co., 294 Wisconsin Avenue, Wash-
EXPERIENCE: ington, D.C. 20013: Promoted improved community
relations with company. Solved customer complaints. Re-
organized product displays. Handled orders. 1980 to 1982.

JT's, 332 Monroe St., Washington, D.C. 20014:
Recruited new clients. Maintained inventory. Developed
direct sales approach. 1977 to 1979.

Functional Resume

GAIL S. TOPPER

136 W. Davis St.	Washington, D.C. 20030	202/465-9821

OBJECTIVE: A professional sales position. . . leading to management . . . in information processing where administrative and technical experience, initiative, and interpersonal skills will be utilized for maximizing sales and promoting good customer relations.

EDUCATION: B.A. in Communication, 1983.
George Mason University, Fairfax, Virginia.

- Courses in interpersonal communication, psychology, and public speaking.
- Worked full-time in earning 100% of educational and personal expenses.

AREAS OF EFFECTIVENESS

SALES/ CUSTOMER RELATIONS: Promoted improved community relations with business. Solved customer complaints. Recruited new clients. Re-organized product displays. Maintained inventory. Received and filled orders.

PLANNING/ ORGANIZING: Planned and re-organized word processing center. Initiated time and cost studies, which saved company additional labor costs and improved efficiency of personnel. Developed and organized technical reference room for more effective utilization of equipment. Created new tracking and filing system for Mag cards which resulted in eliminating redundancy and improving turnaround time.

TECHNICAL: Eight years of experience in operating Mag card and high speed printers: IBM 6240, Mag A, I, II, IBM 6640, and Savin word processor.

PERSONAL: 30. . . excellent health. . . single. . . enjoy challenges. . . interested in productivity. . . willing to relocate and travel.

REFERENCES: Available upon request.

Combination Resume

GAIL S. TOPPER

136 West Davis St.   Washington, D.C. 20030   202/465-9821

OBJECTIVE: A professional sales position. . . leading to manage-
                    ment. . . in information processing where administrative
                    and technical experience, initiative, and interpersonal
                    skills will be utilized for maximizing sales and promoting good
                    customer relations.

AREAS OF EFFECTIVENESS

SALES/   Promoted improved community relations with business.
CUSTOMER   Solved customer complaints. Recruited new clients.
RELATIONS: Re-organized product displays. Maintained inventory.
                     Received and filled orders.

PLANNING/   Planned and re-organized word processing center. Initiated
ORGANIZING: time and cost studies, which saved company $30,000 in
                     additional labor costs and improved efficiency of
                     personnel. Developed and organized technical reference
                     room for more effective utilization of equipment. Created
                     new tracking and filing system for Mag cards which resulted
                     in eliminating redundancy and improving turnaround time.

TECHNICAL: Eight years of experience in operating Mag card and high
                     speed printers: IBM 6240, Mag A, I, II, IBM 6640, and
                     Savin word processor.

EMPLOYMENT   MCT Corporation, Washington, D.C.
EXPERIENCE: Martin Computer Services, Annandale, Virginia.
                     STR Systems, Inc., Washington, D.C.
                     NTC Corporation, Springfield, Virginia.

EDUCATION: B.A. in Communication, 1983
                     George Mason University, Fairfax, Virginia.

                     ● Courses in interpersonal communication, psychology,
                       and public speaking.
                     ● Worked full-time in earning 100% of educational and
                       personal expenses.

PERSONAL: 30. . . excellent health. . . single. . . enjoy challenges
                     . . . interested in productivity. . . willing to relocate
                     and travel.

Resume Letter

136 W. Davis St.
Washington, D.C. 20030
January 7, 19___

James C. Thomas, President
Advanced Technology Corporation
721 West Stevens Road
Bethesda, Maryland 20110

Dear Mr. Thomas:

Advanced Technology's word processing equipment is the finest on the market today. I know because I have used different systems over the past eight years. Your company is the type of organization I would like to be associated with.

Over the next few months I will be seeking a sales position with an information processing company. My technical, sales, and administrative experience include:

- technical: eight years operating Mag card and high speed printers: IBM 6240, Mag A, I, II, IBM 6640, and Savin word processor.
- sales: recruited clients; maintained inventory; received and filled orders; improved business-community relations.
- administrative: planned and re-organized word processing center; created new tracking and filing systems; initiated time and cost studies which reduced labor costs by $30,000 and improved efficiency of operations.

In addition, I have a Bachelor's degree in communication with emphasis on public speaking, interpersonal communication, and psychology.

Your company interests me very much. I would appreciate an opportunity to meet with you to discuss how my qualifications can best meet your needs. Therefore, I will call your office next Monday, January 18, to arrange a meeting with you at a convenient time.

Thank you for your consideration.

Sincerely yours,

Gail S. Topper

Appendix B

RESUME STYLES

The following resume examples reflect different educational and experience levels. The resume on page 223 is for a high school graduate with vocational skills and experience. The resume on page 224 is for a junior college graduate with a non-traditional background. The resume on page 225 is appropriate for a recent B.A. graduate.

The final example, on pages 226 and 227, differs from all others. Especially appropriate for individuals with an M.A. or Ph.D. degree, or for individuals with specialized research, publication, and other production experience, this example includes an add-on supplemental sheet which lists relevant qualifications. The main resume is still one page. The add-on sheet is designed to reinforce the major thrust of the resume without distracting from it.

If we were to select papers for these resumes, we would choose some variation of a white, off-white, beige, light blue, or light grey. We do not recommend other colored papers. It is best to stay with very light and conservative colors. While you should normally stay with black ink, we recommend dark brown or navy blue ink which nicely complement off-white, beige, and grey colored papers. We do not recommend other colored inks.

222

JOHN ALBERT

1099 Seventh Avenue
Akron, Ohio 34522
(322) 745-8271

OBJECTIVE: A position as architectural drafter with a firm specializing in commercial construction where technical knowledge and practical experience will enhance construction design and building operations.

EXPERIENCE: Draftsman: Akron Construction Company, Akron, Ohio. Helped develop construction plans for $14 million of residential and commercial construction. (1985 to present)

Cabinet Maker: Jason's Linoleum and Carpet Company, Akron, Ohio. Designed and constructed kitchen counter tops and cabinets; installed the material in homes; cut and laid linoleum flooring in apartment complex. (1982 to 1985)

Carpenter's Assistant: Kennison Associates, Akron, Ohio. Assisted carpenter in the reconstruction of a restaurant and in building of forms for pouring concrete. (Summer 1981)

Materials Control Auditor: Taylor Machine and Foundry, Akron, Ohio. Collected data on the amount of material being utilized daily in the operation of the foundry. Evaluated the information to determine the amount of material being wasted. Submitted reports to production supervisor on the analysis of weekly and monthly production. (Summer 1980)

TRAINING: Drafting School, Akron Vocational and Technical Center, 1984. Completed 15 months of training in drafting night school.

EDUCATION: Akron Community High School, Akron, Ohio. Graduated in 1983.

PERSONAL: 23. . . single. . . willing to relocate. . . prefer working both indoors and outdoors. . . strive for perfection. . . hard worker. . . enjoy photography, landscaping, furniture design and construction

REFERENCES: Available upon request.

GARY S. PLATT
2238 South Olby Road, Sacramento, California 67342
(712) 564-3981

OBJECTIVE

A position in the areas of systems analysis and implementation of Management Information Systems which will utilize a demonstrated ability to improve systems performance. Willing to relocate.

RELATED EXPERIENCE

Engineering Technician, U.S. Navy.

Reviewed technical publications to improve operational and technical descriptions and maintenance procedures. Developed system operation training course for high-level, nontechnical managers. Developed PERT charts for scheduling 18-month overhauls. Installed and checked out digital computer equipment with engineers. Devised and implemented a planned maintenance program and schedule for computer complex to reduce equipment down-time and increase utilization by user departments. (1982 to 1987)

Assistant Manager/System Technician, U.S. Navy, 37 person division.

Established and coordinated preventive/corrective maintenance system for four missile guidance systems (9 work centers) resulting in increased reliability. Advised management on system operation and utilization for maximum effectiveness. Performed system test analysis and directed corrective maintenance actions. Interfaced with other managers to coordinate interaction of equipment and personnel. Conducted maintenance and safety inspections of various types of work centers. (1979 to 1981)

Assistant Manager/System Technician, U.S. Navy, 25 person division.

Supervised system tests, analyzed results, and directed maintenance actions on two missile guidance systems. Overhauled and adjusted within factory specifications two special purpose computers, reducing down-time over 50%. Established and coordinated system and computer training program. During this period, both systems received the "Battle Efficiency E For Excellence" award in competition with other units. (1976 to 1978)

EDUCATION

U.S. Navy Schools, 1981 - 1985:

Digital System Fundamentals, Analog/Digital Digital/Analog Conversion Techniques, UNIVAC 1219B Computer Programming, and Technical Writing.

A.S. in Education, June 1982:

San Diego Community College, San Diego, California
Highlights:
Graduated Magna Cum Laude
Member, Phi Theta Kappa Honor Society

CHERYL AYERS

2589 Jason Drive
Ithaca, New York 14850   (202) 467-8735

OBJECTIVE:	A research, data analysis, and planning position in law enforcement administration which will utilize leadership, responsibility, and organizational skills for improving the efficiency of operations.
EDUCATION:	<u>B.S. in Criminal Justice, 1987.</u> Ithaca College, Ithaca, New York 14850. • Major: Law Enforcement Administration • Minor: Management Information Systems G.P.A. in concentration 3.6/4.0
AREAS OF EFFECTIVENESS:	<u>Leadership</u> Head secretary while working at State Police. Served as Rush Chair and Social Chair for Chi Phi Sorority. Elected Captain and Co-Captain three times during ten years of cheerleading. <u>Responsibility</u> Handled highly confidential information, material, and files for State Police. Aided in the implementation of on-line banking system. In charge of receiving and dispersing cash funds for drive-in restaurant. <u>Organization</u> Revised ticket system for investigators' reports at State Police. Planned schedules and budget, developed party themes and skits, obtained prop material, and delegated and coordinated work of others during sorority rush. <u>Data Analysis</u> Program in Fortran, Cobal, and RPG II. Analyzed State Police data on apprehensions; wrote report.
PERSONAL:	22. . . excellent health. . . single. . . enjoy all sports and challenges. . . willing to relocate.
REFERENCES:	Available upon request from the Office of Career Planning and Placement, Ithaca College, Ithaca, New York 14850.

MICHELE R. FOLGER
733 Main Street
Williamsburg, Virginia 23572
(804) 376-9932

OBJECTIVE: A manager/practitioner position in public relations which will utilize research, writing, and program experience. Willing to relocate.

EXPERIENCE: Program Development

Conducted research on the representation of minority students in medical colleges. Developed proposal for a major study in the field. Secured funding for $845,000 project. Coordinated and administered the program which had major effect on medical education.

Initiated and developed a national minority student recruitment program for 20 medical colleges.

Writing

Compiled and published reports in a variety of educational areas. Produced several booklets on urban problems for general distribution. Published articles in professional journals. Wrote and presented conference papers.

Research

Gathered and analyzed information concerning higher education in a variety of specialized fields. Familiar with data collection and statistics. Good knowledge of computers.

Administration and Management

Hired and trained research assistants. Managed medium-sized office and supervised 30 employees.

Public Relations

Prepared press releases and conducted press conferences. Organized and hosted receptions and social events. Spoke to various civic, business, and professional organizations.

WORK   ATS Research Associates, Washington, D.C.
HISTORY: Virginia Education Foundation, Richmond, Virginia.
Eaton's Advertising Agency, Cincinnati, Ohio.

EDUCATION: M.A., Journalism, College of William and Mary, 1984.
B.A., English Literature, University of Cincinnati, 1981.

REFERENCES: Available upon request.

SUPPLEMENTAL INFORMATION   MICHELE R. FOLGER

Public Speaking

- "The New Public Relations," New York Public Relations Society, New York City, April 8, 1988.
- "How to Prepare Effective Press Conferences," Virginia Department of Public Relations, Richmond, Virginia, November 21, 1987.
- "New Approaches to Public Relations," United States Chamber of Commerce, Washington, D.C., February 26, 1987.

Professional Activities

- Delegate, State Writer's Conference, Roanoke, Virginia, 1988.
- Chair, Journalism Club, College of William and Mary, 1987.
- Secretary, Creative Writing Society, University of Cincinnati, 1986.
- Co-Chair, Public Relations in the United States Conference, College of William and Mary, 1986.
- Chair, Women's Conference, Junior League of Cincinnati, 1985.

Publications

- "The Creative Writer Today," Times Literary, Vol. 6, No. 3 (September 1987), pp. 34-51.
- "Representation of Minority Medical Students," Medical Education, Vol. 32, No. 1 (January 1987), pp. 206-218.
- "Recruiting Minority Students to Medical Colleges in the Northeast," Vol 23, No. 4 (March 1986), pp. 21-29.

Reports

- "Increasing Representation of Minority Students in 50 Medical Colleges," submitted to the Foundation for Medical Education, Washington, D.C., May 1987, 288 pages.
- "Urban Education as a Problem of Urban Decay," submitted to the Urban Education Foundation, New York City, September 1986, 421 pages.

Continuing Education

- "Grantsmanship Workshop," Williamsburg, Virginia, 1987.
- "Developing Public Relations Writing Skills," workshop, Washington, D.C., 1986.
- "New Program Development Approaches for the 1980's," Virginia Beach, Virginia, 1985.
- "Research Design and Data Analysis in the Humanities," University of Michigan, 1984.

Educational Highlights

- Assistant Editor of the Literary Times, University of Cincinnati, 1981-1982.
- Earned 3.8/4.0 grade point average as undergraduate and 4.0/4.0 as graduate student while working full time.
- M.A. thesis: "Creative Writing Approaches to Public Relations"

Appendix C

EFFECTIVE JOB SEARCH LETTERS

The following types of letters are written in reference to pages 155-167 in the text. In addition, they are related to the resumes appearing in Appendix B.

The resume letters on pages 229 and 230 are designed for the high school graduate (John Albert) and the M.A. degree recipient (Michele R. Folger) in Appendix B. The cover letters on pages 231 and 232 relate to the A.S. and B.A. graduates (Gary S. Platt and Cheryl Ayers) in Appendix B. The approach letters on pages 233 and 234 are designed for the high school graduate (John Albert) in Appendix B and the B.A. graduate (Gail S. Topper) in Appendix A.

Six types of thank-you letters are presented on pages 235-240: the standard post interview, informational interview, response to a rejection, withdrawal from consideration, response to a job offer, and terminating employment.

Resume Letter

1099 Seventh Avenue
Akron, Ohio 34522
August 25, 19 ___

Michael C. Marvis, President
Marvis Construction Company
1121 Jackson Blvd.
Akron, Ohio 24520

Dear Mr. Marvis:

Your recently completed shopping complex on Eighth Avenue is well designed and compatible with the existing neighborhood. I am particularly impressed with how you placed the parking area next to the main access points for the restaurant and theatre complex.

I am especially interested in your work because my background is in architectural drafting. I know good design, and I want to associate with a firm that will fully use my talents. My qualifications include:

- Three years of architectural drafting experience; helped develop plans for $14 million of residential and commercial construction.
- Three years handling all aspects of construction — building and installing cabinets, reconstructing commercial building, pouring concrete.
- Collected and evaluated data for controlling quality of construction.
- Trained as a draftsman.

At present I am seeking an opportunity to use my skills in developing projects similar to your Eighth Avenue shopping complex. I would appreciate an opportunity to meet with you to discuss our mutual interests. I will call your office next week to arrange a convenient time.

I look forward to meeting you.

Sincerely yours,

John Albert

Resume Letter

773 Main Street
Williamsburg, Virginia 23572
November 21, 19 ___

Barbara Thompson, President
SRM Associates
421 91st Street
New York, New York 11910

Dear Ms. Thompson:

I just completed reading the article in Business Today on SRM Associates. Your innovative approach to recruiting minorities is of particular interest to me because of my background in public relations and minority recruitment.

I am interested in learning more about your work as well as the possibilities of joining your firm. My qualifications include:

- research and writing on minority recruitment and medical education
- secured funding and administered $845,000 minority representation program
- published several professional articles and reports on creative writing, education, and minorities
- organized and led public relations, press, and minority conferences
- M.A. in Journalism and B.A. in English

I will be in New York City during the week of December 10. Perhaps your schedule would permit us to meet briefly to discuss our mutual interests. I will call your office next week to see if such a meeting can be arranged.

I appreciate your consideration.

Sincerely yours,

Michele R. Folger

Cover Letter

2237 South Olby Road
Sacramento, California 67342
July 17, 19 —

David Myers
Vice President
Fulton Engineering Corporation
1254 Madison Street
Sacramento, California 67340

Dear Mr. Myers:

Mr. John Bird, the Director of Data Systems at Ottings Engineering Company, informed me that you are looking for someone to direct your new management information system.

I enclose my resume for your consideration. During the past 10 years I have developed and supervised a variety of systems. I have worked at both the operational and managerial levels and know how to develop systems appropriate for different types of organizations.

I would appreciate an opportunity to visit with you and examine your operations. Perhaps I could provide you with a needs assessment prior to an interview. I will call you next week to make arrangements for a visit.

Thank you for your consideration.

Sincerely yours,

Gary S. Platt

Cover Letter

2589 Jason Drive
Ithaca, New York 14850
April 3, 19 —

Sharon A. Waters
Personnel Director
New York State Police Department
892 South Park
Albany, New York 11081

Dear Ms. Waters:

I enclose my resume in response to your November 1 listing in the Ithaca College Placement Office for a research and data analyst with your department.

The position interests me for several reasons. My education and work experience have prepared me for this position. On May 15 I will receive my B.S. degree in Criminal Justice, with specialities in research and data analysis. I am familiar with the New York State Police operations based upon my work in your Albany office this past summer and upon my research on apprehension rates.

The position you outline is one which I feel I can enhance with my technical background as well as my active leadership roles which involve extensive planning, organizing, and communicating. I am a responsible person who is concerned with performance and accountability.

I would appreciate an opportunity to discuss with you how I might best meet your needs. I will call your office next week to inquire about an interview.

Thank you for your consideration.

Sincerely yours,

Cheryl Ayers

Approach Letter

1099 Seventh Avenue
Akron, Ohio 34522
December 10, 19 ___

Janet L. Cooper, Director
Architectural Design Office
RT Engineering Associates
621 West Grand Avenue
Akron, Ohio 34520

Dear Ms. Cooper:

John Sayres suggested that I write to you in regards to my interests in architectural drafting. He thought you would be a good person to give me some career advice.

I am interested in an architectural drafting position with a firm which specializes in commercial construction. As a trained draftsman, I have six years of progressive experience in all facets of construction, from pouring concrete to developing plans for $14 million in commercial and residential construction. I am particularly interested in improving construction design and building operations of shopping complexes.

Mr. Sayres mentioned you as one of the leading experts in this growing field. Would it be possible for us to meet briefly? Over the next few months I will be conducting a job search. I am certain your counsel would assist me as I begin looking for new opportunities.

I will call your office next week to see if your schedule permits such a meeting

Sincerely yours,

John Albert

Approach Letter

136 West Davis St.
Washington, D.C. 20030
October 2, 19 ___

Sharon T. Avery
Vice President for Sales
Bentley Enterprises
529 W. Sheridan Road
Washington, D.C. 20011

Dear Ms. Avery:

I am writing to you because you know the importance of having a knowledgeable, highly motivated, and enthusiastic sales force to market your fine information processing equipment. I know because I have been impressed with your sales representatives.

I am seeking your advice on how I might prepare for a career in your field. I have a sales and secretarial background — experience acquired while earning my way through college.

Within the coming months, I hope to begin a new career. My familiarity with word processing equipment, my sales experience, and my Bachelor's degree in communication have prepared me for the information processing field. I want to begin in sales and eventually move into a management level position.

As I begin my job search, I am trying to gather as much information and advice as possible before applying for positions. Could I take a few minutes of your time next week to discuss my career plans? Perhaps you could suggest how I can improve my resume — which I am now drafting — and who might be interested in my qualifications. I will call your office on Monday to see if such a meeting can be arranged

I appreciate your consideration and look forward to meeting you

Sincerely yours

Gail S. Topper

Thank-You Letter
Post Interview

1947 Grace Avenue
Springfield, Massachusetts 01281
November 17, 19 __

James R. Quinn, Director
Personnel Department
Davis Enterprises
2290 Cambridge Street
Boston, Massachusetts 01181

Dear Mr. Quinn:

Thank you for the opportunity to interview yesterday for the Sales Trainee position. I enjoyed meeting you and learning more about Davis Enterprises. You have a fine staff and a sophisticated approach to marketing.

Your organization appears to be growing in a direction which parallels my interests and career goals. The interview with you and your staff confirmed my initial positive impressions of Davis Enterprises, and I want to reiterate my strong interest in working for you. My prior experience in operating office equipment plus my training in communication would enable me to progress steadily through your training program and become a productive member of your sales team.

Again, thank you for your consideration. If you need any additional information from me, please feel free to call.

Yours truly,

Gail S Toppei

Thank-You Letter
After Informational Interview

921 West Fifth Street
Denver, Colorado 72105
July 18, 19 __

James R. Taylor
Assistant Manager
Associated Financial Advisors
241 Skyline Road
Denver, Colorado 72108

Dear Mr. Taylor:

Joan Karvin was right when she said you would be most helpful in advising me on a career in finance.

I appreciated you taking time from your busy schedule to meet with me. Your advice was most helpful and I have incorporated your suggestions into my resume. I will send you a copy next week.

Again, thanks so much for your assistance. As you suggested, I will contact Mr. David James next week in regards to a possible opening with his company.

Sincerely yours,

John Perkins

Thank-You Letter
Responding to Rejection

1947 Grace Avenue
Springfield, Massachusetts 01281
September 14, 19 __

Sharon T. Avery
Vice President for Sales
Bentley Enterprises
529 W. Sheridan Road
Washington, D.C. 20011

Dear Ms. Avery:

Thank you for giving me the opportunity to interview for the Customer Services Representative position. I appreciate your consideration and interest in me.

Although I am disappointed in not being selected for your current vacancy, I want you to know that I appreciated the courtesy and professionalism shown to me during the entire selection process. I enjoyed meeting you, John Roberts, and the other members of your sales staff. My meetings confirmed that Bentley Enterprises would be an exciting place to work and build a career.

I want to reiterate my strong interest in working for you. Please keep me in mind if another position becomes available in the near future.

Again, thank you for the opportunity to interview and best wishes to you and your staff.

Yours truly,

Gail S. Topper

Thank-You Letter
Withdrawing from Consideration

733 Main Street
Williamsburg, Virginia 23512
December 1, 19 ___

Dr. Thomas C. Bostelli, President
Northern States University
2500 University Drive
Greenfield, Massachusetts 03241

Dear President Bostelli:

It was indeed a pleasure meeting with you and your staff last week to discuss your needs for a Director of Public and Government Relations. Our time together was most enjoyable and informative.

As I discussed with you during our meetings, I believe one purpose of preliminary interviews is to explore areas of mutual interest and to assess the fit between the individual and the position. After careful consideration, I have decided to withdraw from consideration for the position.

My decision is based upon several factors. First, the emphasis on fund raising is certainly needed in your case, but I would prefer more balance in my work activities. Second, the position would require more travel than I am willing to accept with my other responsibilities. Third, professional opportunities for my husband would be severely limited in northwest Massachusetts. Consequently, we would have difficulty maintaining our current lifestyle on my income alone.

I want to thank you for interviewing me and giving me the opportunity to learn about your needs. You have a fine staff and faculty and I would have enjoyed working with them.

Best wishes in your search.

Yours truly,

Michele R. Folger

Thank-You Letter
Accepting Job Offer

2589 Jason Drive
Ithaca, New York 14850
August 19, 19 __

Sharon A. Waters
Personnel Director
New York State Police
Administrative Division
892 South Park
Albany, New York 11081

Dear Ms. Waters:

I want to thank you and Mr. Gordon for giving me the opportunity to work with the New York State Police. I am very pleased to accept the position as a research and data analyst with your planning unit. The position requires exactly the kind of work I want to do, and I know that I will do a good job for you.

As we discussed, I shall begin work on July 1, 19 __. In the meantime, I shall complete all the necessary employment forms, obtain the required physical examination, and locate housing. I plan to be in Albany within the next two weeks and would like to deliver the paperwork to you personally. At that time, we could handle any remaining items pertaining to my employment. I'll call next week to schedule an appointment with you.

I enjoyed my interviews with you and Mr. Gordon and look forward to beginning my job with the Planning Unit.

Sincerely yours,

Cheryl Ayers

cc: Mr. Edward Gordon, Administrator
Planning Unit

Thank-You Letter
Terminating Employment

1099 Seventh Avenue
Akron, Ohio 34522
August 2, 19 __

Mr. James T. McFarland
Chief Engineer
Akron Construction Company
1170 South Hills Highway
Akron, Ohio 34524

Dear Jim:

I am writing to inform you that I will be leaving Akron Construction Company on September 15, 19 __ to accept another position.

As you know, I have developed an interest in architectural drafting which combines my drafting skills with my artistic interests. While I was vacationing in Houston recently, a relative approached me about an opening for someone with my background with a large architecture and engineering firm. I investigated the possibility and, consequently, received an offer. After careful consideration, I decided to accept the offer and relocate in Houston.

I have thoroughly enjoyed working for you over the past two years, and deeply appreciate your fine supervision and support. You have taught me a great deal about drafting, and I want to thank you for providing me with the opportunity to work here. It has been a very positive experience for me both personally and professionally.

I wanted to give you more than the customary two weeks notice so you would have time to find my replacement. I made the decision to relocate yesterday and decided to inform you immediately.

Best wishes.

Sincerely,

John Albert

INDEX

THE AUTHORS

RONALD L. KRANNICH

Ronald L. Krannich is President of Development Concepts Incorporated, a training, consulting, and publishing firm. He has a Ph.D. in political science and public administration from Northern Illinois University. A former university professor, he is a noted lecturer, consultant, writer, and publisher specializing in career management, government, international development, and travel. He has conducted numerous job search seminars and completed several research projects in the United States and abroad. Widely published in major journals and with more than 20 books on career development, government, international development, and travel to his credit, his most recent career books include *Careering and Re-Careering for the 1990s, The Complete Guide to International Jobs and Careers, Salary Success, Find a Federal Job Fast, Discover the Right Job for You, Network Your Way to Career and Job Success, Interview For Success, Re-Careering in Turbulent Times, Moving Out of Government*, and *Moving Out of Education.* He currently resides in Manassas, Virginia.

WILLIAM J. BANIS

William J. Banis is Director of Career Development Services at Old Dominion University. He has an M.A. in speech communication, counseling, and student personnel administration from Penn State University. Currently completing his Ph.D., he has received extensive training in career development from major leaders in the field. A noted consultant and public speaker, he has conducted numerous programs on career development and job placement for professional associations, government agencies, community groups, colleges, and corporations as well as appeared on radio, television, and professional conference panels. He is the co-author of *Moving Out of Education: The Educator's Guide to Career Management and Change.* He currently resides in Virginia Beach, Virginia.

Both authors are available for interviews, training, and consultation. They can be contacted directly through the publisher by writing or calling: Impact Publications, Careers Editor, 4580 Sunshine Court, Woodbridge, Virginia 22192, Tel. 703/361-7300.

CAREER RESOURCES

Call or write IMPACT PUBLICATIONS to receive a free copy of their latest comprehensive, illustrated, and annotated catalog of nearly 1,000 career resources.

The following career resources, many of which are mentioned in Chapter Twelve, are available directly from Impact Publications. Complete the following form or list the titles, include postage (see formula at the end), enclose payment, and send your order to:

> **IMPACT PUBLICATIONS**
> Careers Department
> 4580 Sunshine Court
> Woodbridge, VA 22192
> Tel. 703/361-7300
> FAX 703/335-9486

Orders from individuals must be prepaid by check, moneyorder, Visa or Master-Card number. We accept telephone and FAX orders with a Visa or MasterCard number.

Qty.	TITLES	Price	TOTAL
JOB SEARCH STRATEGIES AND TACTICS			
___	Careering and Re-Careering for the 1990s	$12.95	___
___	Complete Job Search Handbook	$12.95	___
___	Getting Hired	$9.94	___
___	Go Hire Yourself an Employer	$9.95	___
___	Joyce Lane Kennedy's Career Book	$29.95	___
___	Super Job Search	$24.95	___
___	Wishcraft	$7.95	___
___	Who's Hiring Who	$10.95	___
___	Work in the NEW Economy	$14.95	___

Qty.	TITLES	Price	TOTAL
SKILLS IDENTIFICATION, TESTING, AND SELF-ASSESSMENT			
___	Charting Your Goals	$12.95	___
___	Discover the Right Job For You!	$11.95	___
___	Discover What You're Best At	$11.95	___
___	Quick Job Hunting Map	$2.95	___
___	Truth About You	$11.95	___
___	What Color Is Your Parachute?	$18.95	___
___	Where Do I Go From Here With My Life?	$11.95	___
___	Skills for Success	$4.95	___

RESEARCH ON CITIES, FIELDS, AND ORGANIZATIONS

___ American Almanac of
    Jobs and Salaries $13.95 ___
___ California $9.95 ___
___ Career Finder $9.95 ___
___ Careers Encyclopedia $29.95 ___
___ Dictionary of Occupational
    Titles $32.95 ___
___ Encyclopedia of Careers
    and Vocational Guidance $94.95 ___
___ *"How to Get a Job in..."*
    Atlanta, Chicago, Dallas/
    Ft. Worth, Houston, Los
    Angeles/San Diego, New
    York, San Francisco,
    Seattle/Portland, Washington,
    DC ($15.95 or $139.95 for
    set of 9) $139.95 ___
___ *Job Bank Series:* Atlanta,
    Boston, Chicago, Dallas,
    Denver, Detroit, Florida,
    Houston, Los Angeles,
    Minneapolis, New York, Ohio
    Philadelphia, San Francisco,
    Seattle, St. Louis, Washington,
    DC ($13.95 each or $229.95
    for set of 17) $229.95 ___
___ Jobs Rated Almanac $14.95 ___
___ Occupational Outlook
    Handbook $24.95 ___

RESUMES, LETTERS, AND NETWORKING

___ Damn Good Resume Guide $7.95 ___
___ Does Your Resume Wear
    Aprons? $7.95 ___
___ Does Your Resume Wear
    Blue Jeans? $7.95 ___
___ High Impact Resumes
    and Letters $12.95 ___
___ Is Your *"Net"* Working? $24.95 ___
___ Network Your Way to
    Job and Career Success $11.95 ___
___ Perfect Cover Letter $11.95 ___
___ Perfect Resume $10.95 ___
___ Resume Catalog $13.95 ___
___ Resumes That Knock
    'Em Dead $9.95 ___
___ Your First Resume $10.95 ___

DRESS, APPEARANCE, AND IMAGE

___ Color Me Beautiful $17.95 ___
___ Color Wonderful $10.95 ___
___ Dress For Success $9.95 ___
___ Professional Image $10.95 ___
___ Winner's Style $11.95 ___
___ Women's Dress For
    Success $8.95 ___
___ Working Wardrobe $11.95 ___

INTERVIEWS AND SALARY NEGOTIATIONS

___ Five Minute Interview $12.95 ___
___ How To Make $1,000
    A Minute $8.95 ___
___ Interview For Success $11.95 ___
___ Salary Success $11.95 ___
___ Sweaty Palms $10.95 ___

PUBLIC-ORIENTED CAREERS

___ American Almanac of
    Government Jobs and
    Careers (1991) $15.95 ___
___ American Almanac of Jobs
    and Careers With Nonprofit
    Organizations (1991) $15.95 ___
___ Compleat Guide to Finding
    Jobs in Government $14.95 ___
___ Complete Guide to Public
    Employment $15.95 ___
___ Directory of Executive
    Recruiters $34.95 ___
___ Find a Federal Job Fast! $9.95 ___
___ Good Works: A Guide to
    Social Change Careers $17.95 ___
___ How to Get a Federal Job $15.00 ___
___ Invest Yourself: The Catalog
    of Volunteer Opportunities $8.95 ___
___ Profitable Careers
    in Nonprofits $12.95 ___

INTERNATIONAL AND OVERSEAS JOBS

___ Complete Guide to
    International Jobs
    and Careers $13.95 ___
___ Guide to Careers in
    World Affairs $12.95 ___
___ How to Get a Job Overseas $8.95 ___
___ International Careers $12.95 ___
___ International Jobs $12.95 ___
___ Overseas List $13.95 ___

MILITARY

___ From Soldier to Civilian $13.95 ___
___ Re-Entry $13.95 ___
___ Woman's Guide to
    Military Service $10.95 ___
___ Young Person's Guide
    to the Military $17.95 ___

WOMEN AND SPOUSES

___ Careers For Women
    Without College $10.95 ___

___ Relocating Spouse's
Guide to Employment $12.95 ___

COLLEGE STUDENTS

___ After College $11.95 ___
___ College Majors
and Careers $16.95 ___
___ Internships $24.95 ___
___ Liberal Arts Jobs $11.95 ___

JOB LISTINGS

___ Federal Career Opportunities
(6 issues) $37.00 ___
___ Federal Jobs Digest
(6 issues) $29.00 ___
___ International Employment
Hotline (12 issues) $29.00 ___

CHILDREN, YOUTH, AND SUMMER JOBS

___ It's Your Future $11.95 ___
___ A Real Job For You $9.95 ___
___ Teenager's Guide to the Best
Summer Opportunities $18.95 ___

MINORITIES, IMMIGRANTS, DISABLED

___ Black Woman's Career
Guide $14.95 ___
___ Directory of Special
Programs For Minority
Group Members $26.95 ___
___ Finding A Job in the U.S. $8.95 ___
___ Job Hunting For
the Disabled $10.95 ___

EXPERIENCED AND ELDERLY

___ 40+ Job Hunting Guide $10.95 ___
___ Getting a Job After 50 $29.95 ___
___ Success Over 60 $10.95 ___
___ What's Next? $11.95 ___

ALTERNATIVE CAREER FIELDS

___ Business and Management
Jobs $21.95 ___
___ Career Opportunities in
the Music Industry $24.95 ___
___ Careers in Engineering $16.95 ___
___ Careers With Robots $24.95 ___
___ Engineering, Science,
and Computer Jobs $23.95 ___
___ Flying High in Travel $14.95 ___
___ Making It in the Media
Professions $18.95 ___
___ New Accountant Careers $13.95 ___
___ **"Opportunities in..."**

___ Series (145 titles: $12.95
each or $1699.95 set;
contact publisher) $1699.95 ___
___ Outdoor Career Guide $20.95 ___
___ Planning Your Medical
Career $17.95 ___
___ Your Successful Real
Estate Career $11.95 ___

_____

SUBTOTAL   ___

Virginia residents add
4.5% sales tax   ___

POSTAGE/HANDLING ($3.00 for
first title and $.50 for each
additional book) $3.00

Number of additional
titles x $.50 ------------------------------ ___

TOTAL ENCLOSED ------------------ ___

SHIP TO:

NAME _____

ADDRESS _____

_____

_____

[ ] I enclose check/moneyorder for
$ _____ made payable to
IMPACT PUBLICATIONS.

[ ] Please charge $ _____ to my
credit card:

Card # _____

Expiration date: _____ / _____

Signature _____

SEND TO: IMPACT PUBLICATIONS
ATTN: Careers Department
4580 Sunshine Court
Woodbridge, VA 22192

CALL/FAX: Tel. 703/361-7300
FAX 703/335-9486